Equitrekking

Equitrekking

Travel Adventures on Horseback

By Darley Newman

Photographs by Chip Ward

CHRONICLE BOOKS

SAN FRANCISCO

Library of Congress Cataloging-in-Publication Data available.
ISBN: 978-0-8118-6527-2

Manufactured in Hong Kong

Designed by FINE design group

Equitrekking is a registered trademark of Darley C. Newman
and DCN Creative, LLC.

10 9 8 7 6 5 4 3 2 1

Chronicle Books LLC
680 Second Street
San Francisco, California 94107
www.chroniclebooks.com

Contents

Introduction

If it weren't for horses, I never would have been able to *truly* travel. Through riding, I have met a diverse group of people and experienced a slice of their daily lives while exploring the fascinating world that we share.

I feel like a modern-day pioneer when I travel on horseback because it opens a special, intimate window into a land and its people. On each adventure, I spend time getting to know my fellow riders as they show me the very best of their part of the earth. Whether I'm enjoying the abundant fruits of a rainforest on Maui or touring ancient ruins on the remote islands of Ireland, I ride local breeds and travel the terrain that forged the character of both the horses and the people.

My Public Television series, *Equitrekking*, is about these travels on horseback. While our crew shoots video and photographs, I listen, ask questions, and try to learn local riding styles and skills. I hear the sounds of nature and the stories of the people for whom horses are still so much a part of life.

In unfamiliar areas, my senses are heightened and I am hyperaware of the raw beauty of the nature that surrounds me. I do not just pass through a place. I absorb it. Riding into a volcanic crater on Maui, I am conscious of the crunch of cinders beneath my horse's hooves. In Hawaii's Waipi'o Valley, I learn about the horses that helped the locals farm their lush, remote region. Iceland's confident, strong Viking horses, whose shaggy manes protect them from the elements, guard me, too, as I travel through terrain inaccessible by other means. In Doñana National Park in southern Spain, I ride among a herd of red and fallow deer, all of us completely at peace.

Traveling on horseback alongside the locals, whose stories of the land, its history, and their own lives gives each destination its own story, I discover nature in a completely new and refreshing way.

The places that I have visited to produce the *Equitrekking* series and this book are dream destinations. Each trip fulfills another of my wishes. Crossing the Rocky Mountains in Colorado when the wildflowers are in full bloom is like living a dream; so, too, is taking in the bright palette of a California Wine Country sunset in a remote area with the freshest air and the very best view of the Napa and Sonoma valleys, or galloping down wide, golden Irish beaches. Each trip grants me an incredibly blessed feeling, another once-in-a-lifetime experience. This book is based on those travels, and I am excited to share these adventures with you. I hope that these pages take you to places that you have dreamed about seeing and introduce you to the beautiful horses that can allow you to experience the freedom and calm beauty of our natural world. Travel is an adventure that is sometimes best experienced on horseback.

opposite Darley enjoys a beach ride on Jade, a 15-year-old Irish Cob, in Donegal in Northwest Ireland.

page 6 Darley and two local riders enjoy a sunset ride in the West Maui Mountains near Lahaina, Maui.

Chapter 1

The Irish Coast

Donegal•

•The Cooley
Peninsula

Omey Island•

The Connemara Pony
(Dartfield)

The Ring of Kerry

Omey Island

A low fog hangs close to the sand as a small herd of free-roaming cattle, sensing the ebbing tide, make a break from their home on Omey Island toward the Connemara mainland. Their path is made of sand, and for a few short hours each day it's the only bridge connecting this mythical tidal island to civilization.

Omey Island looks out onto the chilly North Atlantic, with rugged Connemara at its back. Locals say that Connemara is the edge of the world and that Omey Island is the "back end of nowhere." It's nearly as far west as you can travel in Europe. Like many destinations in Connemara—Ireland's "Wild West"—Omey's rough terrain is best explored on horseback.

On Omey it's easy to become disoriented and arrive on the edge of a cliff, peering through the fog at the islands of Cruagh and Inishturk in the distance. Winter brings gale-force winds to the island that shift its sand dunes and reshape its landscape. Summers are marked with pink and white wildflowers that form a living blanket underfoot.

There is much to learn about ancient and contemporary Irish history on the island. Celtic crosses in the island's graveyard and recently excavated monastic settlements are juxtaposed with stone houses abandoned since the mid-nineteenth-century Potato Famine and more modern vacation cottages. Before the famine, Omey Island was home to hundreds of people. Today it is home to one permanent resident. A large, dilapidated stone house stands at the end of the sand bridge where the island begins. The largest structure on the island, it marks the bridge for travelers returning to the mainland. During Ireland's Plantation period in the sixteenth and seventeenth centuries, this residence was owned by the Blake family, who were among the many British aristocrats sent by British political and military leader Oliver Cromwell to "settle" Ireland. The ruins of numerous large buildings on the old Blake

opposite Darley and Siobhan look out on the excavation site of St. Feichin's seventh-century Omey monastery. Early Christian burial sites have also been excavated and studied on the north side of the island.

above With its disappearing sand bridge, impossibly green grass, mysterious thick fog, and wild tales of years past, Omey Island is a fascinating place to ride.

pages 10–11 Darley Newman and Siobhan Cazabon of Cleggan Beach Riding Centre pass the remnants of the Blake family's estate on Omey Island, a tidal island in the far west of Conne-mara. Locals like Siobhan know Omey's unpublished history: notoriously harsh absentee landowners, the Blakes were eventually burned out of their house by their tenants. The remaining out-buildings indicate the family's wealth.

property exhibit the wealth of these absentee land-owners. To protest the Blakes' harsh treatment, their tenants set fire to the estate.

The remains of early Christian abbeys and medieval churches stand sentinel for congregations who have long since moved on. Seventh-century Christians, believing that Omey literally was the end of the earth, and therefore closer to God, made this mysterious island their home. The most popular of the island's Christian figures is St. Feichin, who established an abbey here in the seventh century. St. Feichin spread Christianity throughout much of western Ireland, and tales of his supernatural powers abound. Locals and visitors alike leave handmade offerings in his holy well on Omey's western side, whose waters are thought to cure a variety of ailments. Riders may leave an offering of horse hair inside the well beneath the wooden crucifix, before continuing over rolling hills to the nearby excavation site of St. Feichin's church. It is possible to approach the church ruins on horseback but caution is required. At this ancient site, scholars and craftsmen may have once copied manuscripts and sculpted high crosses. In 1981, its thick stone walls were uncovered, and today they lie surrounded by steep, grassy walls, as if dug out of a sand trap.

Still other remnants of Omey's monastic past lie buried beneath the sand, yet to be disturbed. The presence of spirits is alive and well on the island. Perhaps that is why early Christians returned here to be buried—as do many locals today—so that they could remain on Omey Island's sacred ground forever.

top Two curious horses graze in the pasture overlooking St. Feichin's church. There may be other structures beneath these horses' feet that are yet to be uncovered.

above Darley and Siobhan cross the sand bridge to remote Omey Island. Water overtakes the sand bridge twice a day and can rise to the highest point on a horse's back. Cars, too, may get stuck on their way to or from the island.

opposite St. Feichin's Church was only recently excavated. Riders must tread carefully or dismount to get a closer look.

Donegal

Donegal is the Republic of Ireland's northernmost county. One of its main attractions are spectacular wide golden-sand beaches. Riders enjoy the freedom this space provides, and surfers flock to catch large waves in the frigid North Atlantic waters. The beaches of the surf town of Bundoran are a particularly great place to let loose on horseback.

Many people liken the freedom of beach riding to that of flying. Riders on spirited Irish horses soar across Bundoran's sands and into its waters, accelerating from a canter to a gallop and accompanied by crashing waves and the soft beat of hooves on the wet sand. High dunes and sharp cliffs surround the broad Bundoran beaches. Shallow tidal pools cast reflections of the horses and riders that pass, and hoofprints in the sand leave a brief mark of passage in the world.

But Donegal isn't all beaches. Roads and trails wind through vast bogs and expanses of wilderness. These roads hold great significance for the people of this region: they were smugglers' routes between Northern Ireland and the Republic during the Troubles that plagued Ireland in the twentieth century. Locals smuggled everything from chickens to guns on these desolate byways. Today the roads are traveled by riders and hikers making their way through a bit of Irish history.

Surrounded by water, Donegal is joined to the Republic of Ireland only by a small sliver of land. This isolation made life in Donegal different than that in the rest of the Republic. Even the name Donegal means "the fort of foreigners." Though the Troubles have eased, the struggles have not been forgotten by the locals whose stories of hardships haunt those who travel along these smuggling roads.

left top Little back lanes like this one were used as smuggling routes during the struggles between Northern Ireland and the Republic of Ireland. On such roads, riders may hear about the locals' hardships as they view Northern Ireland in the distance.

left bottom Waves lap against the Atlantic shore, with the Blue Stack mountains, so named because of their bluish hue, in the distance. Donegal is frequented for its vast, untamed coastline and golden beaches.

above To get to the beach on horseback, follow the trails winding through rolling sand dunes covered in marram grass, which protects the dunes from erosion and serves as a habitat for many species. Marram grass traditionally has been used as roofing material in houses close to the shore. In the dunes, riders can warm up with a fast trot before galloping on the shore.

opposite The beach town of Bundoran has wide, desolate sands that are ideal for beach riding. Bundoran is a popular destination that became known as the Brighton of Ireland in the early twentieth century.

The Cooley Peninsula

This part of northeastern Ireland lies in the lesser-visited County Louth, the nation's smallest county. Though small, Louth offers a wealth of special treasures. Here trails forged by the great Irish heroes ascend into the Ravensdale Forest, and it is here that the *Táin Bó Cúailnge*, Ireland's greatest epic poem, originated. An Irish Sport horse, a cross between the Irish Draught and the Thoroughbred, known for its athleticism and speed, is an excellent companion on explorations of the Cooley Peninsula, as the trails open up into long, smooth stretches ideal for a good canter or gallop. Riders cross old stone bridges over ravines overgrown with vegetation to find ancient Stone Age circles hidden amid the woods.

The terrain in this part of Ireland is diverse, including natural wetlands and peat bogs. Dark ridges appear next to roads where turf has been cut and laid out to dry for next season. Few still use turf to heat their homes, but the boglands remain popular destinations. They are thriving ecosystems that span hundreds of millions of years.

On the higher mountain trails, the terrain changes. Various shades of brown are replaced by countless greens. Sheep dot the distant meadows and hills like little white cotton swabs. On a clear day, Clermont Carn, the third-highest peak in the Cooley Mountains, allows a view of eight of the thirty-two Irish counties. Here there

are panoramic views of busy Lough Carlingford, the stark granite peaks of the Mourne Mountains, and the rolling green hills of the Cooley Peninsula.

Down the Mourne Mountains in the village of Carlingford, both horse and rider can find rest for the night. The town looks as though it hasn't changed much in hundreds of years. Here one finds the ancient but well-preserved Taeffe's Castle, the Mint, and King John's Castle, all beside a colorful harbor in the shadow of the mountains. Peaceful now, Carlingford suffered Viking raids in the eighth and ninth centuries. Not far across the lough is Northern Ireland. People kayak, windsurf, and boat in the lough's waters and locals enjoy pints of Guinness in the warm pubs of this friendly town, where the Irish spirit is truly alive.

left top Darley on Jesse, a sweet Irish Cob, in Ravensdale Forest. Irish Cobs have long manes, beautiful feathering on their legs and around their hooves, and kind dispositions. Cobs have been carrying travelers for centuries and are excellent trail mounts.

left Riders pass through the cool shade of a beech tree in the almost-magical Ravensdale Forest. Trails follow the route of the *Táin Bó Cúailnge* (The Cattle Raid of Cooley), Ireland's greatest epic poem.

opposite Darley and Niall Connolly rest by an ancient stone circle in Ravensdale Forest. This area of Ireland holds many special sites, best reached on horseback with a local guide. Connolly, the fourth generation of his family in this area, leads riders to its hidden gems.

The Ring of Kerry

There's a reason that County Kerry, on the coast of southwest Ireland, is one of the country's most popular travel destinations: it is absolutely beautiful. The Kerry Way Trail, a trail that winds along the scenic Ring of Kerry driving route on the Iveragh Peninsula, leads riders and walkers past peaceful lakes, some of Ireland's highest mountains, the bright-blue waters of Dingle Bay, and everything in between. Sheep may walk alongside, their backs marked with colorful painted stripes to allow their owners to find them as they roam the yellow gorse and heather-covered hills.

While most people experience the Ring of Kerry by vehicle, the best way to take in the beauty of this area is astride a horse. Instead of looking up at the scenery from a crowded roadside, riders are immersed in it, traveling by idyllic lakes and valleys and venturing high into the mountains to enjoy stunning vistas of the southwestern region as their horses carefully tread the increasingly rocky terrain.

Lough Caragh, a glassy five-mile-long lake surrounded by rolling green mountains, provides a good place to rest or enjoy an on-the-trail snack or picnic. Everywhere one looks, the views are spectacular. Valleys tumble into rivers and lakes below. A few small cottages lie at the base of the valley dissected by Lough Caragh, almost hidden by the trees.

County Kerry was particularly affected by the Potato Famine, during which many people either starved or emigrated from Ireland. Coffin ships, so called because of the deplorable conditions on board, left from two main ports in the southwest, their passengers hoping to find something better in the New World.

Stay clear of the lonely hawthorn trees that stand beside old cottages. They are said to be a sacred meeting place for fairies. According to an old superstition, cutting down this white flowering tree will bring bad luck to you and your family.

Continuing up the trails, riders come to the aptly named Windy Gap beside the summit of Seefin Mountain—no matter the time of year, conditions here are windy. The stony grass trail up to the gap is an old "mass road," which once led to the only Catholic church in the area. Parishioners would walk barefoot, a sign of the hard times, from the village of Glen Car, approximately ten miles away, to attend mass on the opposite side of the Windy Gap. The trek up the road is steep and rocky, so horses must be quite fit to undertake this route.

At the top, small stone fences bisect one's views of verdant fields and valleys. Dingle Bay's brilliant waters and sandy golden beaches shimmer in the distance, backed by the glacier-cut Slieve Mish Mountains across the bay. This is quintessential Ireland.

opposite Aoife O'Sullivan, who leads riders through her family's horseback riding operation, Killarney Riding Stables, rides her horse Alladin on an old mass trail on The Ring of Kerry in Ireland.

top Located in southwest Ireland, County Kerry is known for its beautiful mountains and lakes. Trails wind above Lough Caragh, surrounded by the MacGillycuddy's Reeks mountain range.

above Riders pass the bright-orange roof of an abandoned cottage. During Ireland's Potato Famine, the population of Ireland plummeted as residents died or abandoned their homes. Houses such as this one remain as stark reminders of the island's past.

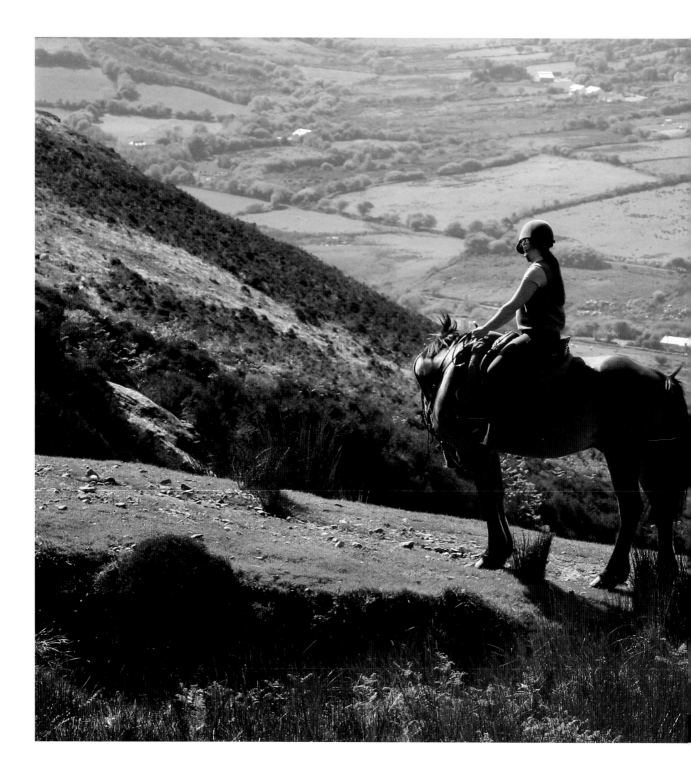

The Connemara Pony

Considered Ireland's only native horse breed, the Connemara pony, has long helped the people of Connemara survive. The region, often described as savage, wild, and uncompromising, is dotted with bogs, rocks, and moors and scoured by the winds and storms of the North Atlantic. Day-to-day life was challenging in the past, but Connemara ponies helped by pulling ploughs through the fields, carrying heavy loads of seaweed and peat, and even carting families to church on Sundays. Many families in Connemara could afford only one horse, a mare that had to be versatile enough to both work throughout the year and carry a foal. Only the toughest ponies survived the grueling daily schedule and the long winters, sustained by the meager vegetation on hillsides and boglands, gifting future generations with the characteristics of strength, stamina, and agility that are prized today.

The Celts may have brought the ancestors of modern-day Connemaras to Ireland, though the ponies' exact origins are unclear. Legend has it that in the sixteenth century, Spanish horses swam ashore to escape a sinking ship. These horses mated with native ponies, and their descendants are the modern-day Connemaras.

Compact, with short legs, strong hindquarters, and a well-proportioned head, Connemaras are surefooted and strong. Able to safely carry small children as well as strong enough to carry adults, these ponies are a resilient and beloved breed.

On a modern journey through Connemara, one will see ponies still grazing the craggy coast, where fingers of land extend into rough waters and the Twelve Bens mountain range rises in the distance. A special treat is to see a herd of ponies running together, manes flowing in the wind in a mesh of gray, black, bay, and brown. At the Dartfield Horse Museum outside Galway, legendary horseman Willie Leahy's hundreds of Connemara ponies graze in herds on lush green parkland. Visitors can get up close to these ponies and, inside the museum, learn about the history of horses in Ireland. Here, too, one can stroll trails on foot or on the back of one of these legendary ponies to explore the park and spot wildlife.

Along the coast, there are other opportunities to ride this dynamic breed along the Connemara Trail, which begins in the mountains and ends at the sea. Here one can relish discovering the region's thatched cottages, historic castles, and rugged beauty on Connemara's native breed.

opposite Connemara ponies graze on rugged banks along the Connemara coast. Many characteristics of modern Connemaras are attributed to the rugged, wild landscapes of the region for which they are named. These hardy ponies are used to being out in the wild, grazing where they can on grass, bog plants, reeds, and whatever else might provide nourishment.

pages 22–23 Aoife O'Sullivan, a local guide whose family owns Killarney Riding Stables, has special knowledge of local folklore and shares some of her favorite stories along the trails. Here Aoife and Darley rest on an old mass road while taking in the green Irish countryside. Decades ago, barefoot worshippers walked this road from the village of Glen Car, ten miles away, to reach the local Catholic church.

right top Connemaras rest after grazing at the Dartfield Horse Museum. Gray and dun are the predominant hues of Connemara ponies, but brown, bay, black, chestnut, palomino, and roan are also breed colors.

right middle Visitors on foot or on horseback can see Connemara ponies of all ages and colors at the Dartfield Horse Museum, which chronicles the history of horses in Ireland and offers trail rides through the area.

right bottom The Connemara pony is a versatile breed. Frequently used in competitions, this pony is prized for its natural jumping ability. Connemara ponies reach maturity at age five and can live into their thirties.

Chapter 2

The Irish Countryside

County Clare

- The Irish National Stud (Kildare)
- Mount Juliet Estate (Conrad)

Mount Juliet Estate

One of Europe's great sporting estates, Mount Juliet's fifteen hundred acres of gardens, woodland, rolling fields, and sculpted decadence stand out amid the countryside of County Kilkenny in southeastern Ireland. To ride at this grand eighteenth-century country estate is to ride in the footsteps of eccentric earls and ladies, lavishly dressed members of high society, and the famous racehorses that were born and bred here. As one of the few intact estates in Ireland, Mount Juliet is a special reminder of a bygone era.

Entering the gates and driving toward the Georgian manor house, which today welcomes guests, one may feel ensconced in a staid setting, but this is not the case and has never been so. Mount Juliet was founded by the Earl of Carrick around 1758 and named after his wife. The earl's descendents inhabited the property until 1914, when Sir Hugh McCalmont purchased the estate. Later McCalmont's grandson Victor would inherit control with his wife, Bunny.

Until the 1980s, Mount Juliet was Bunny and Victor's private residence, complete with a staff of a hundred.

To say that this couple lived the life of Gatsby is to put it mildly. Seven-day parties were a common occurrence, as was a guest or two ending up in the lily pond adjacent to the main manor house. Eventually the immense expense of running the estate became too much for Bunny and Victor. Before it began operating as a hotel in 1989, it was one of only a few working estates in Ireland and the only one in Kilkenny. Mount Juliet is rare in that it has survived many of Ireland's hardest times, including the Potato Famine.

Today the resort prides itself on its world-class fishing, horseback riding, and golf. Visitors can fish with local legend Billy Townsend and hear tales of the estate's glory days from a man who has worked on its stud farm, played in the band that entertained during the McCalmonts' parties, and still works on the property. Most of the staff who once ran this great manor house are gone, but it's the remaining colorful characters such as Townsend, along with the well-kept house and grounds, who make visitors feel as if they are guests

of the departed McCalmonts, dancing at one of their extravagant parties, dressing for cricket, or riding in the hunt.

At the stables, the Kilkenny hounds, who are used for area foxhunts and have been on the estate since the 1920s, bark loudly as riders mount sturdy Irish Sport horses or Thoroughbreds to take a leisurely tour of the grounds. Both breeds are good for jumping on Mount Juliet's cross-country course and riding in hunts. Fit riders may arrange to join in an Irish hunt through Mount Juliet's Equestrian Centre, gaining special access to this traditional sport. As one rides past the main manor house, where roses cascade down the walls and frame the entranceway and a calm lily pond beckons, one hopes that someone will take a photo, as this is truly a picture-perfect setting.

Trout and salmon are prevalent in the fast-flowing River Nore, which runs through the property. Guests don waders and venture into its cool waters, looking up at the large gray manor house and the purple flowers blooming along the stone bridge that leads to the estate's stud farm, Ballylinch Stud. In 1914, Hugh McCalmont's son Dermot McCalmont founded Ballylinch Stud when he retired his award-winning racehorse, the Tetrarch, here. The "Spotted Wonder," so called for his unusual white-spotted gray coat, had won many races, including the Royal Ascot, a high-profile race that began in 1711 and remains one of the top races in the United Kingdom.

Ballylinch Stud still produces award-winning racehorses. Staying in the main manor house, guests may gaze at the horses from across the river or get a closer look on a tour of the stud. Equestrians may watch the horses frolic in the fields beside them as they ride along the River Nore. A few cattle graze with stately young horses and foals in pastures beside the water. This close access to these pricey racehorses is but one perk of staying at the estate. Such is the beauty of Mount Juliet: guests feel that they have joined a club more exclusive than any with velvet ropes. Gracious, luxurious Mount Juliet remains a gem and a historic landmark in the countryside of Ireland.

opposite Instructor Eleanor Dwan rides White Henry, an Irish Draught horse, and Darley rides Harold, an Irish Sport horse, into the cool waters of the River Nore. Irish Draughts were originally used on the country's farms, and Sport horses, commonly a mix of the Thoroughbred and the Irish Draught, are popularly bred as competition horses. Both breeds are known for their wonderful temperaments.

pages 26–27 Riders at An Sibin Riding Centre in County Clare enter a fairy-tale-like setting as they pass the duck pond on the way to the 300-year-old farmhouse lodge.

top Roses drape the walls of the eighteenth-century manor house, where guests may stay during their visit to Mount Juliet Estate. The estate is located outside the town of Kilkenny in southeastern Ireland.

above Riders cross the old stone bridge above the River Nore, known for its abundant wild Atlantic salmon and brown trout. Equestrians may take a leisurely tour of the grounds or hone their skills on a cross-country jumping course.

The Irish National Stud

County Kildare is Irish horse country, the nation's own Lexington, Kentucky. Located just south-west of Dublin, this county's green pastures are home to some of the world's fastest racehorses. Exclusive stud farms dedicated to breeding take advantage of the area's mineral-rich soil, which is said to make the bones of Irish horses very strong. Here horses are trained at the Curragh Racecourse, which hosts Ireland's five biggest horse races, and the public can get close up to award-winning Thoroughbreds at a renowned Thoroughbred breeding farm, the Irish National Stud.

The Stud dates back to the early 1900s, when Colonel William Hall-Walker, a wealthy Scotsman and equestrian, purchased the farm and began to breed Thoroughbreds. Many people thought that Hall-Walker was eccentric. He installed skylights in the stalls so that the horses could look up at the moon and stars. He used astrology and horoscopes to dictate which foals were sold and which were kept. No matter how bizarre his methods may have seemed at the time, they worked. From 1904 to 1914, Hall-Walker bred seven horses that went on to win the country's top races. In 1916, he passed the Stud to the British government, which continued to breed horses here until 1945, when the farm was given to the Irish government.

Visitors today can learn about the history of horses and horse racing in Ireland at the Stud's Irish Horse Museum. Guided tours of the property introduce top breeding stallions such as Invincible Spirit, a sleek bay champion sprinter whose stud fees would put a dent in your pocketbook. In the springtime, the season's new foals awkwardly walk and run in green fields alongside their mothers. These young horses are just getting used to their legs, which at birth are almost the size of an adult horse's. Foals attempt to crane their heads down to the grass to eat like their mothers, but they must nurse during their first few weeks. Miraculously, a newborn horse usually stands up within an hour of birth and can run a day later. This developmental characteristic is essential for horses in the wild. They are prey animals, so being able to flee from danger is their greatest defense.

No visit to the Stud would be complete without a stroll through its Japanese Gardens, among the finest such gardens in Europe. They were devised by Colonel Hall-Walker and his famous Japanese gardener, Tassa Eida. Laid out over a four-year period in the early twentieth century, the gardens are yet another example of Hall-Walker's eclectic taste. Pathways lined with pagodas, vibrant flowers, and streams take visitors through various stages of life, including engagement, marriage, and death. Many a bridegroom has proposed on the bright-red bridge that overlooks the lily pond.

opposite Visitors to the Stud can enjoy the tranquility of one of the finest Japanese gardens in Europe, where a path guides visitors through the various stages of life. The red Bridge of Life leads travelers into the Garden of Peace and Contentment.

right top The spring is a good time to observe foals at the Stud. Mares and their foals reside in paddocks along the Tully Walk. Seeing young horses is the highlight of many visitors' tours.

right bottom Darley gets a rare chance to get close to a young horse at the Irish National Stud in Kildare. This Thoroughbred will be groomed by its owners, who hope that it will become a top racehorse.

County Clare

On the west coast of Ireland, just south of Connemara, County Clare encompasses many of the dramatic landscapes of Ireland, such as the Burren, a desolate, rocky land dotted with archaeological sites, and the Cliffs of Moher, high coastal cliffs offering dramatic views of the Atlantic. The rest of the county, among the more rural parts of Ireland, offers visitors the chance to immerse themselves in nature.

At An Sibin Riding Centre in the foothills of the Slieve Aughty Mountains, visitors enjoy pristine Irish nature as well as true Irish hospitality. Hosts Nicola and Bertie Cummins welcome guests into their carefully refurbished three-hundred-year-old farmhouse. Sitting beside a turf fire with a pint of Guinness or glass of wine amid old stone walls and antiques, while outside white ducks waddle to the small pond, visitors find themselves in an idyllic setting.

Mornings begin with large Irish breakfasts. Though a picnic lunch is served on the trail, visitors frequently can't resist the plentiful morning supply of hearty meats, eggs, cheese, and stiff Irish tea. Days are spent riding to ancient Celtic sites such as Oisín's and Grainne's Grave, a Neolithic dolmen named after an old Irish legend and located in the townland of Bohatch. Dolmens are ancient burial tombs consisting of a large capstone supported by three or more stones. No one knows how the ancients were able to lift and place the heavy capstones. It's very peaceful up in these hills on the way to the dolmen. Riders overlook the River Shannon, the longest river in Ireland and the site of many Viking conquests, where colorful boats and the occasional fisherman make their way along river.

To get closer to Oisín's and Grainne's Grave, riders must ride into the boglands. Here, horses' hooves sink into the soft, moss-covered earth as they climb to the site. This dolmen has never been excavated. Its contents and true story remain a mystery, but riders may listen to local guides tell the legend as they gaze at the ancient structure. In Ireland, many dolmens are found in County Clare, making it no less special when riders stumble across one and are able to open up their imagination to the past.

After a day on the trails, nights come to life at local pubs in the small village of Mountshannon, where everyone knows one another intimately but newcomers are nonetheless welcome. County Clare is known for its vibrant music and arts culture, and its pubs are alive with musicians on fiddles, tin whistles, and flutes mixing improvisation with traditional Irish songs.

opposite Riders pass a Neolithic dolmen, an ancient tomb. Ireland's west coast holds many dolmens, including this one in County Clare. This dolmen has not been excavated; who and what are buried here is a mystery.

right top Nicola Cummins, who with her husband owns An Sibin Riding Centre, offers a warm smile on a country lane nestled amid heather-covered boglands overlooking Lough Derg and the River Shannon.

right bottom Horses at An Sibin usually are not kept inside barns or stalls but are left out to enjoy the Irish countryside, ensuring happy horses. Each morning of their weeklong stays, riders venture out to catch the mounts that will be theirs.

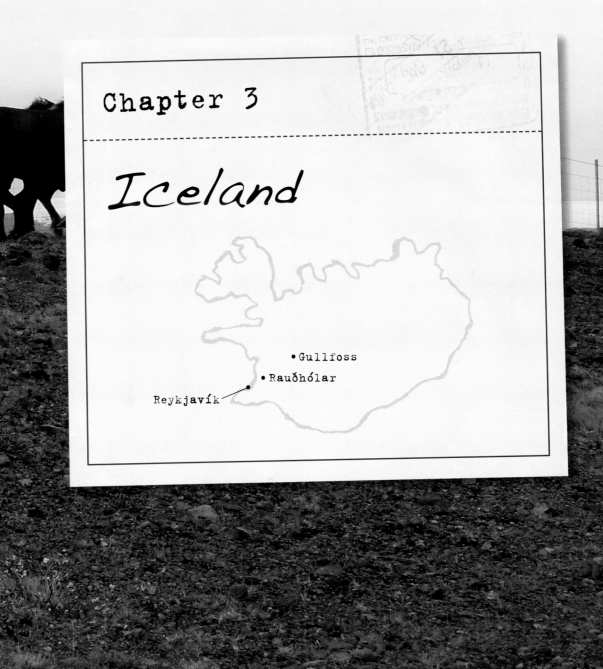

Chapter 3

Iceland

- Gullfoss
- Rauðhólar
- Reykjavík

Reykjavik and Beyond

Iceland, in the north Atlantic Ocean just south of the Artic Circle, is called the land of fire and ice, home to spewing geysers, roaring waterfalls, giant glaciers, and pure nature in all of its beautiful fury. With summers of almost constant sunlight and winters blanketed in darkness, Iceland is a fascinating country of extremes. It is also the land of the Icelandic horse. A source of national pride, this ancient breed has survived over a thousand years in isolation in tumultuous landscapes.

Vikings settled Iceland in the ninth century, bringing horses and other livestock that helped them to cultivate the land, explore, and survive. In Norse mythology, horses were owned and ridden by gods and goddesses, and the Icelandic sagas describe Viking warriors who chose to be buried with their noble steeds. Throughout Icelandic literature, the horse is depicted as a beast of burden, a soldier's partner, and a prized possession. Until the early twentieth century, horses were the sole mode of transportation around the country's rugged lava fields. Even today, Icelandic horses are used to travel the highlands and other areas inaccessible by any other means, and horses are still considered part of the family.

Icelandic horses may be prized for their stamina, but their physical appearance also draws attention.

Icelandics' coats come in myriad colors—chestnut, brown, bay, palomino, gray, and on and on. Big, bushy manes sprout from their compact, muscular bodies. Though they are pony-sized, Icelandics are referred to as horses, most adamantly so by Icelanders themselves. These small, hardy horses pack some might. They also possess the remarkable ability to move in ways distinct from other horses. Icelandic horses can walk, trot, and canter like other breeds, but their extra gaits—the *tölt* and the *skeið*, or pace—make them special.

The *tölt*, a four-beat gait that is similar to a running walk, is very smooth for riders, who, instead of bouncing in the saddle, can glide along with their horses. A favorite way for Icelanders to demonstrate this even gait is to ride along while carrying a pint of beer and not spill a drop. The *skeið* is a faster gait in which the legs on the same side move together. There is a clear moment of suspension when all four legs are off the ground, making the horse look as if it were flying. Not all Icelandics can pace, but those that can pace are said to be five-gaited. The *skeið* is a racing gait, reaching speeds up to thirty miles per hour.

Visitors to Iceland can count on observing these speedy horses at one of the many Icelandic horse competitions in and around Reykjavík, the capital city. People of all ages ride in competitions as well as for pleasure. It's a big part of national life and culture. On weekends, riding clubs come alive as children and adults gather for horse shows, where visitors are welcomed. Observers will kindly explain the intricacies of the shows and maybe even invite you for a coffee afterward.

At Íshestar Riding Tours' riding centre, about a fifteen-minute drive from downtown, riders can safely learn how to ride an Icelandic horse inside a ring before heading out on a longer trek. Some people have compared Iceland's terrain to the surface of the moon. Its landscapes have been cut by giant glaciers and charred by molten lava. In fact, NASA sent Apollo astronauts to Iceland to prepare them for missions to the moon. Upon first encountering this terrain, one may think it a treacherous place to ride, but Icelandic horses have no

opposite Icelandics are one of the purest breeds of horses in the world, having been kept in isolation in Iceland for over one thousand years. These Viking horses have thick manes that protect them from harsh weather and stocky, strong bodies that get them through rugged terrain.

above Darley test-rides an Icelandic horse through a lake outside of Reykjavík. For the most part, Icelandic horses are very willing to move forward and go fast. A true thrill for riders.

pages 34–35 Horses run through rocky lava fields during the horse drive. In such terrain, one can appreciate the nimble Icelandic breed.

problem navigating the rocky and rough landscapes. They have adapted to the land after traveling here for more than a thousand years and are very sure-footed.

Hundreds of years ago, Icelandic settlers were having trouble surviving and cut down almost all the country's trees, burning them to keep warm. After years of erosion, the Icelandic people must work hard to ensure that any trees they now plant stay in the ground. Without the shield of forests, the wind can blow pretty hard, but this is another thing that the horses are completely used to. It's the riders who must bundle up.

By traveling through these harsh landscapes, one can begin to understand how the Icelandic horse developed the strong and versatile attributes for which it is so prized today and why the Icelandic people relied upon these horses to survive. The Icelandic horse is called "the most useful servant" by Icelanders, who cherish their horses as a national treasure.

top left A young rider races on an Icelandic horse in a competition just outside of Reykjavík. Traditional Icelandic saddles have long side panels and relatively flat seats. This style of saddle allows riders to distribute their weight more evenly and adjust as the horse changes gaits and allows the horse a good range of movement. The stirrups, which are larger to accommodate bigger boots, are worn longer. This keeps the riders' leg under their seat, so that they are balanced in the saddle.

top right Horses are a major part of Icelandic culture. On weekends, children and adults gather for horse shows at riding clubs around Reykjavík. These shows, open to the public, are a good stop to see the small but mighty Icelandic horse in action.

opposite At Íshestar Riding Tours' stables outside of Reykjavík, one can learn how to ride an Icelandic horse in the ring and on nearby trails. Here Einar Johannsson and Darley ride through a lake by a small forest before heading to the lava fields.

Rauðhólar

Just outside Reykjavík, Rauðhólar, or the Red Hills, is an ethereal area of deep red pseudocraters that are more than 4,600 years old. Pseudocraters form when hot lava hits water, causing an explosion of steam. The steam may be composed of carbon dioxide or hydrogen sulfide, and as the gasses are forced to the surface, they tear jagged holes in rock and displace sediment, effectively reshaping the land into unusual, often violent looking formations. Besides Rauðhólar, these volcanic cones can also be found on Mars, making riding here truly memorable. Equestrians such as champion rider and trainer Sigurbjörn Bárðarson, known the

Rauðhólar

J ust outside Reykjavík, Rauðhólar, or the Red Hills, is an ethereal area of deep red pseudocraters that are more than 4,600 years old. Pseudocraters form when hot lava hits water, causing an explosion of steam. The steam may be composed of carbon dioxide or hydrogen sulfide, and as the gasses are forced to the surface, they tear jagged holes in rock and displace sediment, effectively reshaping the land into unusual, often violent looking formations. Besides Rauðhólar, these volcanic cones can also be found on Mars, making riding here truly memorable. Equestrians such as champion rider and trainer Sigurbjörn Bárðarson, known the

world over as Diddi, or "the Golden Rider," train horses here because of the challenging terrain.

To train Icelandic horses, many people ride them outside the confines of a ring in wilderness areas. Icelandic horses are very smart and often find training drills monotonous, so trekking out is a good way to keep their attention. Another training method is to ride amid large herds of Icelandics, so that the horse grows used to listening to and being around other horses and riding long distances.

Many Icelanders attribute the character of their horses to the way they are raised. As prey animals, horses have a fight-or-flight instinct, but for over a millennium, Icelandic horses have been isolated on an island without natural predators. Since they have little to be afraid of, their flight instinct is thought to be undeveloped, and Icelanders say that their horses think before running away from challenging or menacing situations. Icelanders have tried to strengthen the breed by breeding only the strongest horses with the best dispositions.

Centuries ago, the Icelandic government made it illegal to import foreign horses to Iceland and declared that once an Icelandic horse is taken out of the country, it can never return. This has kept the Icelandic breed pure and free from disease. This creates an interesting situation for people such as Diddi, who competes riding Icelandic horses throughout the world. If an Icelander brings a horse out of the country to compete, it must then be sold. This means that some of the best Icelandic horse competitions can be seen only in Iceland, because that is where riders keep their best horses.

Riders venture out from nearby private stables to ride at Rauðhólar. In order to ride here, one must know a local with horses or arrange a session with an area trainer like Diddi. Riding through pools of water to cliff shelves and along steep inclines at Rauðhólar, one can experience the energy of the Icelandic horse. This area is like an obstacle course and exercise session for the horses and riders. Horses use their muscles to walk as their feet and legs sink into the cinder soil.

In many sections of Rauðhólar the ground feels like sticky quicksand, but the horses trod through it. Over the course of an outing, riders grow more confident and adjust their bodies to stay balanced. Moving up and down steep inclines, equestrians tilt forward and backward in the saddle. Splashing through pools, riders may lift their legs to avoid chilly waters. It's all part of the experience of riding in this interesting area.

Visitors to Rauðhólar will find accommodations and diversity in nearby Reykjavík, where ample nightlife is available to those who wish to stay up late, and shopping and restaurants are plentiful.

opposite Icelandic horses, which have a well-honed sense of direction and are very sure-footed, are a source of immense pride for the Icelandic people. As Diddi says, "When you cannot see anything and you are lost, usually you just give the reins to the horse and he brings you out of the wilderness. He is so important for the nation."

above Diddi demonstrates how full of energy, yet calm, Icelandic horses are by standing atop his horse. Though these horses are pony-sized, they can easily carry adults—in fact, calling them ponies is offensive to Icelanders.

Gullfoss Horse Drive

Staying on an Icelandic horse farm for a holiday is a wonderful way to experience life in the countryside and a traditional Icelandic horse drive. During these drives, riders follow the speed of the herd, who often move quickly through lava fields and green valleys, past rivers and waterfalls. Visitors are accompanied by spirited Icelanders and fifty or more horses in this unique adventure. Various equestrian tour companies in Iceland, including Íshestar Riding Tours, book riders on these farm holidays throughout Iceland.

Riding with large herds of horses is a custom in Iceland. Because they must cover vast distances, Icelanders often ride one horse while leading another, so that when the ridden horse tires, they can switch mounts and keep going at a good pace. During the summer, when it may be light out almost twenty-four hours a day, the Icelandic people take advantage of the sunlight by organizing frequent drives. Though drives today are held more in the spirit of tradition than out of necessity, they are still a very good way for Icelanders to train their horses and transport them to new summer pastures. In Iceland, horses usually spend their first few years in the wild with other horses. They are not ridden or trained until they are about four years old, later than many other breeds. Icelanders believe that this helps horses develop their individual characters, grow physically strong, and become accustomed to the country's wide-open terrain.

Outside Reykjavík, near Iceland's famous Geysir, neighboring farmers round up their horses for a weekly horse drive to Gullfoss, an area of spectacular waterfalls that cascade into a canyon in southwest Iceland. On the drive, riders may travel along a horse path that lines the Ring Road, the only highway that circumnavigates the country. Though it's the main highway, cars yield to horses here. In the lava fields, the horses almost instinctually navigate the rocks and low shrubs at high speeds. Riders may see the giant glacier Langjökull far in the distance. Approximately 11 percent of Iceland is covered in glaciers, and Langjökull is the country's second largest.

On other horse drives, riders may also venture into the highlands. The isolated interior is home to most of Iceland's glaciers and to desertlike expanses of gravel, gray sand, and tundra. In this area, a *varda*, a road sign made by a pile of rocks, was historically the only way to navigate. One could stand by a *varda*, spot the next one in the distance, and know where to go. Modern-day riders may use GPS, but they still relish the feeling of navigating in the wild.

Off the Ring Road, beside one of Iceland's deep canyons, the scenery becomes more diverse. Cliffs drop hundreds of feet to bluish-gray water flowing from highland glaciers. When they reach Gullfoss, riders witness the power of nature, listening to the roar of these enormous waterfalls.

opposite Farm holidays allow travelers to experience life on an Icelandic farm. Äsa Dalkarls (middle) and her husband, Hjalti Gunnarsson (front), both local farmers and guides, lead Darley on a cliff ride to spectacular scenery alongside a river formed by runoff from a glacier in the highlands.

right On the Ring Road, the main highway and only road that circumnavigates Iceland, it is not uncommon for horses to stop traffic. In this horse-friendly country, the road has both a paved route for cars and a dirt trail alongside it for horses.

Chapter 4

Spain

• Segovia

Sevillá

Doñana National Park •

Jerez de la Frontera

Sevillá

The capital of Spain's southern region of Andalusia, Sevillá is a vibrant city on the Guadalquivir River. The city pulses with the energy of flamenco dancers; locals gather at tapas bars; and a distinctive Roman, Moorish, and early Christian history and architecture enliven its streets. Cortijo El Esparragal, a historic estate, is just outside Sevillá and welcomes visitors as if to a friend's home. Decorated with art and antiques, many with a bullfighting theme, this beautiful retreat invites a small number of guests to experience life on a working farm and to enjoy a variety of activities, including the unusual opportunity to ride prize-winning Andalusian horses.

This Spanish breed, with its long, flowing mane, expressive eyes, and high-stepping walk, has been the preferred mount of kings and queens, cowboys and warriors throughout history, and today both equestrians and horse lovers in Spain and around the world cherish them. Riding them in their native land reveals the beauty, versatility, and courage for which they are prized.

Horses and cattle are raised on the grounds of El Esparragal, a farm that is almost self-sustaining. Dining in the adjoining restaurant, one is likely to enjoy fresh fruits and organic vegetables, including oranges and olives grown right on the property, milk from its more than one thousand dairy cows, and tender beef from its approximately four hundred *retino* cattle, the ancestors of Texas longhorns. Visitors may swim in the quiet pool surrounded by cypress and tall palm trees and manicured gardens. There's black bass fishing, hunting, and carriage rides in addition to riding. Some visitors choose simply to relax in the cobbled courtyard, listening to the birds chirp beneath bright blue skies. Others explore the main house, taking in the varied art and antiques in its drawing room and chapel.

Most Andalusian horses are gray or white, but others are bay, chestnut, or black. The approximately thirty Andalusians at El Esparragal have won numerous awards in horse shows around Spain, making for well-trained mounts. In the stables, riders are paired up with

a horse that is fitted with a *vaquero* (cowboy) saddle, traditionally used to work cattle. It is fashioned to mould to the horse's back and has large, rectangular steel stirrups that protect the rider's feet from bulls' horns and the brush that one may encounter when working on ranches in Andalusia. The soft sheepskin seat is designed for comfort during many hours in the saddle.

As one rides out from the stables, the main building of El Esparragal looks austere yet inviting, with its stark white façade and traditional ceramic-tiled tower. Violet-colored flowers billow from Roman-arched windows. Part of what is now the main hotel was once a monastery for the order of the Jerónimo monks. The small chapel, built by monks in the 1600s and adorned with an eighteenth-century rococo altarpiece, is now used for services and the occasional wedding.

Archaeological history abounds both inside and around the grounds of El Esparragal, including Roman ruins, an Arab mill, an early Christian Visigoth temple, and a Roman aqueduct. Nearby, bulls are situated in their paddocks. Riders may venture inside and play games on horseback. It may sound dangerous, but these bulls are relatively tame and plump, as they are raised for food, not bullfighting. Farther afield, riders follow trails in a Mediterranean forest or view the ruins. In the bullring, skilled horsemen gracefully demonstrate traditional methods for separating cattle from the herd, artfully wielding *la garrocha*, a long pole, in a fashion similar to the way ropes are used by cowboys in the American West.

Only fifteen minutes from El Esparragal, Sevillá's nightlife beckons visitors to dance, eat, and enjoy life. Getting lost in this city is easy, but that's part of the fun. Whether you're exploring Sevillá on foot or its surroundings on horseback, it's best to take things at a Spaniard's pace—relax and enjoy.

opposite Juan Gallego, a trainer at Cortijo El Esparragal, and Darley ride Andalusian horses. Darley's mount is a mare named Vanidosa. In Spain, it is common for breeders to roach, or shave, the manes of mares and foals.

above An architectural gem in southern Spain, El Esparragal's main building's Roman-arched windows and tiled tower welcome visitors to relax and experience history, culture, and award-winning Andalusian horses.

pages 44–45 On the edge of the park, the rare Retuertas horses can graze in the marshes beside the town of El Rocío. The Retuertas are a threatened, wild breed that lives in Doñana National Park. Thought to be one of the oldest breeds of horses in Europe, scientists are studying the Retuertas to discover their lineage and history.

Doñana National Park

This wild and varied destination is on the coast of southern Spain, where the Atlantic Ocean meets the Guadalquivir River delta. Visitors can venture through its three ecosystems—marshes, forests, and vast sand dunes—all within a few hours. Listed as a UNESCO World Heritage Site, Doñana is one of the largest parks in Europe. Bird watchers and animal lovers flock here to see endangered species such as the rare Iberian lynx and Spanish imperial eagle, as well as the variety of other birds that nest, breed, and rest in the safety of Doñana.

Doñana National Park has long been recognized as a special place. In the thirteenth century, part of the area was set aside as a hunting reserve by the kings of Castille, who were attracted by its abundance of game. The park is named after one of the duchesses of Medina Sidonia, Doña Ana de Silva y Mendoza, who built a residence here; the area came to be known as "the forest of Doña Ana," or Doñana. It was established as a national park in 1969.

Though tourists are welcome to visit the park, much of it is off-limits in order to protect the environment. Jeep tours are a popular way to discover the land, as is hiking its trails. Riders, too, can hit the beach and trails surrounding the park, taking in the area's natural beauty on Andalusian horses.

Park guards on horseback grant an insider's tour of lesser-trod areas of Doñana. From the stables, narrow trails wind through dense forests of pine and Mediterranean scrublands containing rosemary, red lavender, and thyme. Partridges, storks, herons, and turtle doves nest in cork oak forests. Out of the forest, the trails open up to a clearing where fallow and red deer travel in herds. Visitors also may glimpse wild boar, badgers, rabbits, otters, and the Egyptian mongoose. Each season brings something new to Doñana. During the winter, more than half a million waterfowl descend, escaping the cold of Northern Europe. For these migrating birds, Doñana is a stop en route to wintertime refuge in Africa. In springtime, colorful flowers bloom in its marshes.

As riders draw closer to the beach, the terrain changes from flat land to sets of rolling, sugary dunes partially covered in coarse grass. Closer still to the shore, the dunes become much larger, some reaching over 100 feet high. Some are stationary, while others move. The mobile dunes are slowly creeping inland, swallowing pine forests as they travel. The beaches in this area are quiet, pristine, and wide. Riders may spot the tracks of the many mammals that roam the park, and seagulls and oystercatchers play by the shore at the tail end of Europe.

On the edge of the park, the whitewashed pilgrimage town of El Rocío borders Doñana's marshes, where feral horses graze. The horses, the Retuertas, are thought by some scientists to be one of the oldest breed of horses in Europe. The town's streets are made of sand in order to accommodate horses. In the spring, almost one million people flock to El Rocío, many on horseback or in carriages, for the Romería del Rocío pilgrimage, which celebrates the Virgen del Rocío, the Virgin of the Dew.

opposite Darley takes a dip in the Atlantic Ocean on a beautiful white Andalusian horse named Figo. In Spain, riders can sink into soft sheepskin saddles, ideal for long days on the trails.

right top Wildlife in the park is abundant. Tourists often spot red deer, such as this stag resting in the middle of sea grass. Only the stags grow antlers, which they shed annually.

right bottom Darley rides with Juan Luis, a guard at Doñana National Park, who grants a special tour of lesser-visited areas. The two ride by a forest of verdant trees, which will soon be covered by mobile sand dunes.

Segovia

North of Madrid outside the historic city of Segovia, hundreds of horses populate the golden-brown countryside of Yeguada Centurión, one of the largest breeding farms for Andalusian horses in the world. This grand Spanish farm prides itself on raising prizewinning Pure Spanish horses in an environment that mingles the high-tech with the historic, and it welcomes visitors to appreciate its beautiful horses and tour its grounds.

The breed standards and characteristics for Pure Spanish Horses that are still recognized today were defined in the sixteenth century, when Pure Spanish Horses became unified as a breed in Spain. Flush with the wealth that Spain was enjoying from the New World, King Philip II decided to breed the noblest of Spanish horses. He founded the Spanish horse's stud book, the official record of the breed's pedigree, at the Royal Stables in Córdoba and began to select and breed stock fit for royalty. In the following years, these prized horses were in great demand as cherished gifts and assets of European monarchs.

In 1912, a new stud book was founded in Spain. The Spanish began referring to their special Andalusians, those that are purebred Spanish horses, as P.R.E., or *pura raza española*. These special Andalusians are still a national treasure in Spain, and a major part of

Spanish equestrian culture. At Yeguada Centurión, visitors can meet over six hundred Pure Spanish horses spread among more than 2,200 acres of golden grasslands.

Visitors may tour the Monastery of San Pedro de las Dueñas, a thirteenth-century Benedictine monastery that has been carefully restored. Out in the fields, hundreds of horses graze beneath beech and juniper trees with the sweeping Sierra de Guadarrama mountains in the background. Horses are released into this bucolic setting at about six months old, and remain outside until they are about three and a half years. This ensures that the horses grow strong and confident before they begin training. The award-winning Rondeno IX, a thirteen-year-old bay stallion, is one of the farm's top horses; for two years in a row, he has been recognized as the champion stallion of Spain. Visitors frequently wish they could take these beautiful horses home after a stop at this top breeding farm, which offers a rare opportunity to see spectacular horses in a typical Spanish setting.

opposite Hundreds of horses populate Yeguada Centurión, one of the world's largest breeding farms for Andalusian horses. Visitors may tour the farm and view horses in its pastures.

right top A Spanish rider dressed in sixteenth-century attire finishes a training session inside Yeguada Centurión's arena. Many horses bred on the farm excel in dressage and go on to win competitions.

right bottom The peaceful countryside outside the city of Segovia about one hour north of Madrid is set against the Sierra de Guadarrama mountains. Oak trees line the pastures of the lower slopes. Scenes like this are common on country drives and the drive to Yeguada Centurión.

Jerez de la Frontera

This city, in the sunny southern region of Andalusia, is known for its sherry and its horses. In November, its streets come alive with the Feria del Caballo, a celebration of Spanish horses through competitions, parades, and dancing, but any time that one visits this city, one feels the rhythm of the horse. The Royal Andalusian School of Equestrian Art, Real Escuela Andaluza del Arte Ecuestre, a school that trains some of the best horses and riders in Spain, educates visitors on the history of equestrian culture in Spain and showcases the aptitude of its best horses and riders through performances and practices that are open to the public. Another stop for horse and wine lovers is Yeguada Real Tesoro, a winery that also breeds rare black Andalusian horses.

Jerez's architecture is a composite of neoclassical, baroque, and gothic. On the well-manicured grounds of the Royal School, the equestrian center lies beside a nineteenth-century baroque-style palace designed by Charles Garnier, who designed the Paris Opéra. Inside the equestrian center, visitors may watch horses and riders train.

They may also attend *How the Andalusian Horses Dance*, an equestrian ballet. Riders in eighteenth- and nineteenth-century-style costumes perform various types of country and classical dressage as well as emulate the traditional way to work with horses on Spanish cattle ranches. Dressage is a discipline in which horses are trained to carry out various movements based on slight cues from their riders. Horse and rider appear melded together, as if in a dance. During the *piaffe* the horse trots in place. In the *pirouette*, the rider bends his horse and the horse moves in a stationary circle, turning around his hind end. As one watches the horses, with their long, full manes and arched necks, glide through their balletlike strides and step high in the air, one can appreciate the bond between horse and rider and the years of training both must undergo to attain such harmony.

Set to Spanish and classical music, the show is choreographed to include carriages forming figure-eight patterns around the ring, barely avoiding collision. Drivers may only use their hands, voice, and whip to drive the horses, making carriage driving a more challenging sport than meets the eye. Another highlight of the performance is the *capriole*, when the horses leap into the air in a stunning feat of athleticism.

Just down the road, Yeguada Real Tesoro, a traditional sherry bodega that dates back to 1760, invites guests to visit award-winning pure black Andalusian horses and tour its facilities. A bodega is a winery where sherry, a sweet fortified wine, is produced. Jerez's special, chalky *albariza* soil acts like a sponge, soaking up winter rain and storing it to keep grapevine roots well nourished all year long. Although there are bodegas all over Spain, this is special because of its rare horses. A small museum of antique carriages is situated beside the horses' stalls.

Compared to other colors of Andalusian horses, black horses are unusual and thus of great value. These horses, once used to pull carriages in funeral processions, became associated with death and bad luck and so fell out of favor. But today they are prized for their color. The approximately sixty champion horses here, bred and raised for competitions, exhibitions, classical dressage, and carriage pulling, are all named after sherries and brandies.

Antiques and art from the seventeenth and eighteenth centuries adorn the walls inside the bodega, giving each room an aristocratic feel. Touring the cool, dark cellars, visitors find barrels that have been aged from 60 to over 120 years. The largest cellar contains over 25,000 barrels of sherry. In one of the smaller cellars, holding over 2,000 barrels of the very dry *fino* sherry, the barrels are signed by famous visitors or friends of the bodega's owner. Classical music that has been specially composed to help the sherry age lulls visitors as they taste the driest *fino* or the very sweet Pedro Ximinex, with its hints of caramel, nuts, and toffee. Drinking sherry and seeing wonderful horses—there are few better ways to spend an afternoon.

opposite A magnificent horse statue stands in a charming town square of Jerez de la Frontera in the province of Andalusia. Jerez, known for its horses and sherry, is an ideal city to explore on foot.

right A rider bows to crowds in the 1,600-seat arena during a performance at the Royal Andalusian School of Equestrian Art in Jerez. Famed rider Don Alvaro Domecq Romero helped found the school in the 1970s.

Chapter 5

The Georgia Coast

- Sea Island
- Jekyll Island
- Cumberland Island

Cumberland Island

Roughly the size of Manhattan, Cumberland Island lies off the coast of southern Georgia. Unlike Manhattan, though, it is rich in wildlife and diverse ecosystems. Nature rules on this barrier island. Wild horses roam its fertile salt marshes, maritime forests, and more than seventeen miles of golden-brown beaches. Most of the few cars seen here are rusty antiques, abandoned along with the island's Gilded Age mansions. The call of modern technology wasn't answered here; large landowners and the National Park Service have tightly regulated growth, and the island is no more developed now than it was in the early twentieth century. Traveling here affords a window into the island's complex and fascinating history and a special chance to observe horses in the wild.

Cumberland Island's known human history is thought to date back four thousand years to the Native American tribes, who hunted here. The Spanish are thought to have brought the first horses in the 1500s, when they built forts and missions on the island. Later, from the mid-eighteenth to mid-nineteenth centuries, horses and cattle were among the island's chief products, along with corn, indigo, and cotton. During those plantation days, slaves greatly outnumbered their white owners on the island.

After the Civil War, life changed throughout the South, and the island's slave economy ended. Newly

wealthy Northerners took an interest in Cumberland in the mid-nineteenth century. One of these families, the Carnegies, Pittsburgh steel magnates and devoted equestrians, acquired most of the island and imported various breeds of horses with an eye toward improving their island stock. It is said that they even brought a white stallion from a Russian czar and several mustangs from the American Southwest to the island. The horses that now roam Cumberland are a blend of the Carnegie stock, horses of other plantation owners, and Spanish steeds of years past.

Cumberland Island was established as a national seashore in 1972 and is managed by the National Park Service. As a result, the number of people coming to and from the island each day is restricted. Travelers can take a ferry from nearby St. Marys, a charming town on the St. Marys River, and hike island trails or take a guided tour led by a naturalist or park ranger. But no matter how one discovers Cumberland, be sure to visit the special places where the island's wild horses may be seen.

Wild horses graze and drink well water near the stone pillars of Dungeness, a once lavish mansion on one of the island's few grassy areas. Dungeness was built by Catherine Greene Miller, the widow of Revolutionary War hero General Nathanial Greene. Catherine, who some believe inspired Eli Whitney's cotton gin, had the

top A foal cranes down as it emulates its mother eating grass near the Greyfield Inn. Hiking is the best way to take in the island's natural wonders. With a lot of ground to cover, visitors may choose to camp on the island or stay at the Greyfield Inn.

opposite Wild horses can be found on East Coast islands and in pockets throughout the United Sates. Chincoteague Island's ponies, off the coast of Virginia, are the more famous. Feral horses also populate Sable Island, Canada, and Shackleford Banks, North Carolina.

above Cumberland's beaches are striking, revealing slanted trees and large sand dunes. One may spot a sea turtle or dolphin here. Armadillos, wild turkeys, and bobcats may also be seen on the island.

pages 54–55 Travelers navigate through driftwood on the northern end of Jekyll Island, one of Georgia's "Golden Isles," a lovely setting for beach rides.

thirty-room, four-story "tabby" mansion built. Tabby is a mixture of water, sand, oyster shells, and ash—all readily available materials on the island—that at the time was often used for building in coastal Georgia. Later the Carnegies built a larger mansion on the Dungeness foundations, adding a squash court, forty outbuildings, a golf course, and manicured gardens. In 1959, Dungeness was destroyed by a fire, leaving behind only ruins whose thick walls are today being reclaimed by dense vines.

Other remarkable structures on the island include the Georgian Revival–style mansion Plum Orchard, also built by the Carnegies, and the one-room First African Baptist Church, where John F. Kennedy Jr. and Caroline Bessette were wed. Their reception was held at the Greyfield Inn, the only place to stay on the island.

Situated on the Atlantic flyway, Cumberland Island is a haven for wildlife, with migratory birds, bobcats, deer, alligators, herons, hummingbirds, loggerhead turtles, and even armadillos. Giant live oaks dripping with Spanish moss provide travelers a bit of shade as they meander along trails lined with saw palmettos and slanted trees—forced by wind into bonsai-like shapes—nestled among sea oats. The beaches are constantly eroding and sprouting new life. Sand dunes can reach over forty feet tall. Wild horses roam the sands, munching on the vegetation that helps to stabilize the dunes. The beaches of Cumberland are dynamic, wide, and devoid of people, making them and the island itself a very special oasis.

The small, elegant Greyfield Inn was built in 1900 as a wedding present for Lucy and Thomas Carnegie's daughter Margaret, and it is filled with family antiques. There are no telephones in the rooms, and the inn itself has very limited communication with the mainland. Its long, deep porch offers rocking chairs and swings stuffed with oversized pillows, all excellent spots to relax with a book or a glass of sweet tea during the heat of the day. Its lawn is a popular grazing spot for horses, which can be watched in comfort from the high porch. In the chill air of the evening, baskets of blankets are within arm's reach. Dinners are served

by candlelight, and afterward guests are free to make themselves at home and fix a drink, a simple gesture that invites them to open up and mingle easily. A visit to the inn and its island home will take you back to more graceful, peaceful times.

opposite top A favorite grazing spot for horses is the lawn of the Greyfield Inn. Built in 1900 by the Carnegie family, the small, elegant inn is the only lodging on the island.

opposite bottom Another popular spot for the horses to graze is by the ruins of Dungeness mansion. Dungeness has a long history of decay and revival.

above Naturalist Fred Whitehead, who has lived on the island for quite some time, leads travelers to the best places for spotting horses.

Sea Island

A barrier island off the coast of Georgia, Sea Island is known as one of Georgia's "Golden Isles." Since 1928, it has welcomed generations of prominent families. Calvin Coolidge, Henry Ford, Eugene O'Neill, Dwight D. Eisenhower, and wealthy industrialists all were drawn to Sea Island's grand, traditional setting. Today world leaders still visit the island, which hosted the G8 Summit in 2004.

The Cloister, originally a small family inn planned by Howard Coffin, founder of the Hudson Motor Company in Detroit, is now an elegant Spanish-style establishment. It offers more than 150 guest rooms and many luxurious resort amenities, such as world-class golf, live music at dusk by the sea, and horseback riding on the beach.

At the nearby stables, riders can take lessons or head straight to the sands for nature rides. Passing over the Black Banks River, riders will find wooded trails through a maritime forest that offers a rich diversity of bird life, including nesting osprey. Beyond the forest are wide, secluded beaches. This is one of only a few special areas on the East Coast where riders can enjoy the freedom of beach riding.

Riders cantering along the shore may spot pods of dolphins, loggerhead turtle nests, and a wealth of seashells for collecting. Beside trails through the dunes, vital vegetation thrives and thickens, and rare red-billed oystercatchers and tiny fiddler crabs scurry amid delicate white flowers. (Beware: these tempting, fragrant perennials are actually stinging nettles!) Explorers may also find many plants that have been used for medicinal purposes throughout history, such as the toothache tree, properly known as the prickly ash.

Naturalist guides lead riders on eco-tours to Sea Island's tidal salt marshes, which are rich primary nursery grounds for plants and animals, including blue crabs, shrimp, and oysters, and also protect the island from offshore storms. At the banks of the tidal creek, riders may spot great blue herons and egrets over the spartina grasses, all natural wonders best viewed from horseback.

top A bagpiper plays music at dusk by the sea at the Lodge at Sea Island. Families have visited to experience Sea Island traditions since the 1920s.

above Naturalist Stacia Hendricks leads Darley through Sea Island's interdune habitat, pointing out plants and animals of the tidal Low Country.

opposite Darley and Stacia canter on Sea Island's wide beaches. Stacia's horse is named Effie and Darley's mount is Charlie, a large Belgian Draft horse from the island stables.

Jekyll Island

Jekyll Island's reputation as a vacation getaway began in 1886, when the wealthy and powerful Rockefellers, Pulitzers, Morgans, and Vanderbilts established the island as their exclusive winter vacation getaway. This barrier island still welcomes vacationers, but today anyone can enjoy this millionaires' playground.

Visitors ride on Driftwood Beach at the northern end of the island, navigating among the giant roots and limbs of live oaks and pine trees. These skeletal remains create a hauntingly beautiful setting for a beach ride. The lighthouse on nearby St. Simons Island is visible in the distance, and horseshoe crabs, mermaid purses, and colorful shells line the shore at one's feet. Off the beach, trails wind through a cool maritime forest.

In the 1930s, Jekyll Island and its club were winter destinations for tycoons who enjoyed hunting and horseback riding. Populations of pheasants, turkeys, quail, and deer were stocked for shooting from horse-back. The Great Depression and World War II spelled the end of the old Jekyll Island Club, but the club, and the 240 acres on which it sits, is now a National Historic Landmark that is continually undergoing restoration.

Today visitors can stay at the club, whose wide veran-das, wraparound porches, lofty ceilings, and ninety-three fireplaces convey a feeling of grandeur. Many of the surrounding mansionlike cottages built by members in the early 1900s are now museums, open and intact for touring guests. These opulent homes reveal their former inhabitants' elegant manner of living, and cause one to wonder what secrets lie within the parlor rooms and porches of Jekyll Island.

Limits on the amount of land on the island that can be developed have allowed a significant bird and animal population to thrive in the protected habitats of salt marshes, maritime forests, and miles of beaches. Rich in wildlife, dramatic seashore, and well-restored historic sites, Jekyll Island invites riders and non-riders to enjoy a decadent history in a beautiful, natural place.

opposite Darley soaks in the beauty of Jekyll Island's Driftwood Beach on Pretty Boy, a Paint horse with a laid-back island demeanor, along with a fellow rider.

right top Wood storks perch high in the trees by one of Jekyll's marshes. Bird watching is a popular activity on this island. Much of its land is undeveloped, allowing plants and animals to thrive.

right bottom One of many mansion-size "cottages," which were once winter homes for privileged families such as the Rockefellers, Pulitzers, and Vander-bilts, in Jekyll Island's 240-acre National Historic Landmark District.

Chapter 6

The Carolinas

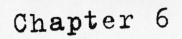

• The Biltmore

Cherokee

• Daufuskie Island

Daufuskie Island

Amid the shade of a maritime forest on Daufuskie Island, South Carolina, riders begin a journey back in time. This windswept barrier island was inhabited hundreds of years ago by the Cusabo Indian tribe. Around the tribe's original encampment, sharp-eyed visitors may spot relics from the period, such as rose quartz arrowheads, pottery, and archaeological ruins. Treasures lie deep in the forest beside the Cooper River, where the summer heat is not so brutal.

From around the time of the Civil War until recently, Daufuskie Island was home to a considerable population of Gullah, descendants of slaves brought to the United States from Africa. Much of the island is now part of the Daufuskie Island Resort, which caters to the small population of island residents and to visitors. Besides golf, tennis, horseback riding, and the spa, guests enjoy relaxing on uncluttered beaches. Accommodations include beach cottages, villas, or the antebellum-style Ocean Front Inn.

Many people have now read of Daufuskie, the centerpiece of Pat Conroy's book *The Water Is Wide*, in which he relates his formative experience teaching African American children in a one-room schoolhouse here.

Daufuskie is about eight square miles in area, with beaches, trails, and dirt roads. To get here, visitors take a forty-five-minute ferry ride from Hilton Head Island. The ferry does not transport cars, making golf carts, horses, and horse-drawn carriages a popular way to get around. At Daufuskie's sunny yellow equestrian center, riding lessons are available, as are lessons in driving an antique surrey carriage. Riding options are oriented toward the English style, though Western-style riding is available. Daufuskie also permits beach riding.

On horseback, riders venture down an unpaved road past a large bald eagle's nest, one of many birds of prey on the island. Beyond pastel-colored houses, tall oak and pine trees back the beaches. The sand holds the remains of shells and broken tree limbs. Here riders have the chance to canter and gallop, taking their horses toward the breaking waves.

Off the beach, Daufuskie's many trails and unpaved roads wind around the island. These are also ideal for exploring on horseback. A dirt road leads riders past the island's white wooden First Union African Baptist Church, which dates back to 1881. Farther on, riders encounter the small red-brick Silver Dew Winery, once owned and operated by Arthur Burns, who made his wine from island grapes and fruit. Dirt trails pass tall pine trees to the banks of the Intracoastal Waterway and the Cooper River, higher ground where the Cusabo may have once lived. Small boats motor along the water that separates Daufuskie from the mainland, which is so close and yet feels a world away.

opposite Visitors pass pastel-colored houses on their way to beach rides on lush Daufuskie Island, with its many unpaved roads and wooded lanes ideal for exploring on horseback.

pages 64–65 Riders venture along a forest path at the Biltmore, where there are approximately eight thousand acres and more than eighty miles of trails.

top Daufuskie's wide, quiet beaches offer travelers the chance to ride fast or take it easy. Tall oaks and pines create an unusual beach setting where riders can search for seashells and breathe the salty air as they cruise the shore.

right Trails wind through a maritime forest to an area inhabited hundreds of years ago by the Cusabo Indian tribe. Here riders can dismount to treasure-hunt for arrowheads and other archaeological remnants around the tribe's original encampment.

Cherokee

Great Smoky Mountain National Park rests on the border of North Carolina and Tennessee. It is bounded to the south for fifteen miles by the Cherokee Nation, home to the Eastern Band of Cherokee Indians, who are primarily the descendents of Cherokee who stayed in this region after 1838, refusing to go west to Oklahoma on what became known as the Trail of Tears. The Smoky Mountains have been home to these strong people for more than a thousand years, and here the Cherokee still ride horses and celebrate their cultural history by continuing the traditions of their ancestors.

In the 1540s, Spanish explorer Hernando de Soto came through these mountains, bringing horses, tools, and other livestock that changed the way the Cherokee lived and worked. In the 1720s, the Cherokee began to breed horses and developed large herds. It is thought that Cherokee women used horses to gather firewood in the winter when the men were away hunting. Horses also helped the Cherokee expand their trade routes; their use as packhorses garnered them the name *sogwili*, which means both "horse" and "pack."

Visitors to the town of Cherokee can ride trails in the Great Smoky Mountains, visit a replica of an eighteenth-century village to learn about traditional life in the area, and attend performances at which the Cherokee tell their stories of the mountains and their history. The Cherokee believe that they are stewards of the land—they are here to protect it, along with their profound history and culture.

Riding out from the park's Tow String Horse Camp with Cherokee guides, riders will encounter trails that are rocky and sometimes steep. Altitudes within the park can range from eight hundred to over six thousand feet. Tennessee Walking horses, with their special smooth gait, are the preferred mounts of many in these mountains. Much of the park is shaded in old-growth forests where mosses and rare species thrive. After many challenging hills, a shaded trail opens up beside a swift-flowing but shallow river where horses can drink mountain spring water among hundreds of yellow butterflies. Spring brings vibrant wildflowers, while summer welcomes colorful mountain laurel, azalea, and rhododendron.

At Oconaluftee Indian Village, a replica of a Cherokee village of 250 years ago, the scents of burning pitch pine and baking bean bread waft amid winding dirt trails that lead to log cabins with bark-shingled roofs. Here Cherokee practice traditional arts, such as pottery making, canoe building, and basket weaving. Visitors can imagine Cherokee life of yesteryear during cold mountain winters when warm blankets of beaver or buffalo hide were laid atop oak-framed beds and families gathered around slowly burning fires. The village and its traditions attest to the endurance of Cherokee life in these mountains; a stroll here reveals both the hardships they faced and the natural bounty they enjoyed, as well as the deep roots that continue to bind today's Cherokee to these mountains.

The Cherokee kept their horses high in the mountains and away from their villages; because they had no fences, the Cherokee feared the horses might run through their villages, and the women, in particular, did not want horses trampling their gardens. Since horse stealing was a problem during that time, the Cherokee began marking their horses. The horse greatly changed life for the Cherokee people, as it has for so many peoples throughout history, and tribal members today still value their mounts, riding the trails and celebrating horses through song and dance. At an outdoor performance of "Unto these Hills," colorfully dressed Cherokee perform the traditional "Horse Dance" as their finale, giving thanks to the horses that have helped them so much.

opposite top Bud Smith, a member of the Eastern Band of Cherokee Indians, and his horse cool off in a stream in the Great Smoky Mountains.

opposite bottom Tribal member Forrest Parker escorts a group on Tennessee Walking horses that he has trained along shaded trails in the Great Smoky Mountains. The breed's special gait allows them to move smoothly through rocky terrain. Tennessee Walking horses were the first breed to share their name with a U.S. state.

The Biltmore

Visitors can saddle up and explore over eighty miles of Appalachian trails winding through the eight-thousand-acre Biltmore Estate in Asheville, North Carolina, much as guests of George Vanderbilt did during the Gilded Age. George, the grandson of wealthy industrialist Commodore Cornelius Vanderbilt, founded the estate in the 1880s, picking the site for, among other things, its stunning Blue Ridge Mountain views.

The name "Biltmore" is a combination of the name Bildt, the Dutch town from which old Vanderbilt's ancestors came, and the Old English word *more,* which means "upland rolling hills." As a young bachelor,

George Vanderbilt had lofty goals when he began plans for the Biltmore Estate. Envisioning a grand European estate, he modeled Biltmore after a French château. In 1889, construction began, using hundreds of workers and massive amounts of limestone. With the help of Frederick Law Olmsted, the landscape designer known for designing great urban landscapes such as Central Park, and the famous American architect Richard Morris Hunt, the house would be one of the most advanced and innovative of its time.

After only six years, the mansion encompassed more than four acres of floor space, 250 rooms filled with art and antiques, an indoor pool, and a bowling alley.

Guests enjoyed the newest and best of everything, including Thomas Edison's new lightbulbs, central heating, and two elevators. Their horses had the best of everything, too. The twelve-thousand-square-foot stable at the north end of the house held various spaces for tack, saddles, harnesses, twenty carriages, and twenty-five horses, and it had fully functioning electricity and plumbing. Farther afield, the historic horse barn housed more horses and mules. The barn and its blacksmith shop were a hub of activity and central to the Biltmore's working farm.

The nation was impressed with the Biltmore. During World War II, the National Gallery of Art in Washington, D.C., stored many priceless works in the Biltmore for safekeeping. Today these works have been returned to the museum, but countless other priceless works owned by the Vanderbilts remain. The Biltmore is the largest private home in the United States and, generations after its building, it is still family-owned and -managed.

Olmsted strived for a serene setting in much of the estate, and his approach is echoed in the modern-day care of its horses. Trainers practice natural horsemanship, a method of communicating with and understanding horses. Riders bring their own horses or ride one of the Biltmore mounts to venture along the French Broad River, which flows from North Carolina into Tennessee. Guests may stay on the Biltmore property at the luxurious Inn on Biltmore Estate, which has spectacular views of the surrounding mountains and allows easy access to all of the property's offerings. The Inn comes alive during the holidays and riders may wish to schedule their stay around a special equestrian center clinic. Riding through wooded trails and meadows, visitors can view the great house and one of America's greatest legacies.

Chapter 7

Virginia

Marriot Ranch • • Middleburg
• The Virginia Gold Cup
(Warrenton)

• Kelly's Ford

Marriott Ranch

Rolling grasslands stretch as far as the eye can see. Longhorn cattle graze in flower-filled meadows, and rugged cowboys ride miles of trails. Though this may sound like the American West, it actually lies fewer than sixty miles outside Washington, D.C. Marriott Ranch, in the foothills of the Blue Ridge Mountains, is not your typical Virginia getaway, or your typical Marriott. Instead it spreads out over 4,200 acres, with more than 1,500 head of cattle, and offers ample opportunity for riding at an all-American ranch chock-full of history.

These rugged lands reminded Marriott founder J. W. Marriott Sr. of his native Utah, and he purchased the ranch as a private retreat in 1951. In later years, Roy Rogers and world leaders including Presidents Eisenhower and Reagan visited the ranch to experience life on the range. The ten-room Inn at Fairfield Farm, the main house on the ranch, is now open to the public, offering guests a chance to experience life in rural Virginia.

James Markham Marshall, brother of the first chief justice of the United States, built the stately red-brick Federal-style inn in 1814. Each of its rooms has working fireplaces and luxurious bedding. Upon arrival, guests are handed a glass of wine instead of a key. The giant antique keys to the doors are a bit unwieldy, so one of

opposite Wooded trails lead through streams on rides at Marriott Ranch. This part of Virginia hunt country has a distinctively laid-back Western feel.

above Horses at Marriott Ranch mill about in a paddock, before a morning trail ride. Paints, Appaloosas, and quarter horses are the predominant breeds at the ranch, where horses must have strong bones and good feet in order to thrive on the rocky trails through mountains and valleys.

pages 72–73 Riders pass through aptly named Paradise Valley on a trail ride at Marriott Ranch.

the friendly innkeepers helps guests to their rooms. In 1939, a Belgian baroness escaping the Nazis lived in what's now called the Baroness Cottage, adjacent to the main inn. Families can stay in her quirky white wooden abode, with its cozy Western decor.

The ranch runs parallel to Skyline Drive, a scenic road that threads its way through Shenandoah National Park. During colonial times, this land was owned by Thomas, sixth Lord Fairfax, the Baron of Cameron, a member of the British aristocracy who inherited more than five million acres in northern Virginia (many places throughout the region, including the city of Fairfax, bear his name). It was Lord Fairfax who inspired a young George Washington to begin a career as a land surveyor. As a young apprentice, the future president may have surveyed the lands where Marriott Ranch now rests.

The land here hasn't changed much since Fairfax's time. Tree-covered Rattlesnake Mountain rises in the distance. Cows graze beside the Rappahannock River, which cuts through the property. From the stables, riders cross sloping grassy fields to dirt trails that wind through miles of shady pine forest. An old stone wall from the 1800s lines the trail that leads riders alongside picturesque streams to Paradise Valley, a favorite spot for cattle to graze, which looks like it could be in Switzerland. Wildflowers carpet the

hill where longhorn cattle—more often denizens of Texas—and their babies pasture.

During the Civil War, James E. Yates, who would later purchase the ranch, sold its cattle to Southern and Northern troops, receiving his payment in gold and becoming a very wealthy man. The cattle that graze today on the thousands of acres of land serve the same functions as they did in the 1800s, including helping to maintain the ranch's vast extent of grassland.

As one crosses through the rolling hills on horseback, it might be easy to forget that this ranch is in Virginia if it weren't for the knowledge of the area's exuberant local guides, whose grasp of history help riders envision the characters who traveled through this land. Other attractions beckon as well. Not far from the farm, the small town of Flint Hill welcomes locals to dine in a cozy tavern. Area vineyards have seen a recent renaissance and there is plenty of antiquing to do—that is, if you decide to get out of your Western saddle and step away from this bit of America's West in the East.

top The spirited horses at Marriott Ranch, a working farm in Hume, Virginia, are appropriate for riders of any skill level. Guests can join cattle drives, picnic rides, and other adventure packages at this Western-style ranch.

opposite Franklin, a 12-year-old Appaloosa, has been at Marriott Ranch for a long time and is the perfect mount for adults and children alike. Appaloosas are known for their unique coat patterns, which may have leopard-like spots and splashes of color.

The Virginia Gold Cup

Fall and spring are prime seasons for equestrian events in Virginia, when weekends are crowded with foxhunts, steeplechases, races, and shows. One of the oldest organized steeplechases in the United States and a premier social event of the spring, the Virginia Gold Cup challenges riders to race through a course of timber and brush fences in a test of courage and endurance for both horse and rider. Tens of thousands of spectators gather each May to watch the Cup's Thoroughbred horses and brightly dressed jockeys line up in the grassy fields of Virginia's Piedmont.

The steeplechase is thought to have originated in Ireland in the eighteenth century when two friends held a race to settle an argument over whose horse was best. The highest points in the area were church steeples, so the friends raced each other to a steeple, crossing the countryside's natural obstacles, such as ditches and fences, along the way. In Virginia, steeplechasing may date back to colonial times. The Gold Cup began in 1922 as a competition between U.S. Army officers and others who were keen to race.

The Gold Cup's four-mile obstacle course is challenging and sometimes results in spills for horses and riders. On this full day of (usually) seven races, during which horses must combine speed with good jumping ability, spectators are allowed unusually close to the course, soaking up the noise of thundering hooves and the rush of excitement as jockeys dash to the finish line.

Although the races are the heart of the Cup, fashion, tailgate parties, and dogs are also major elements. Many men get festive in pink shirts and pants, while ladies don spring dresses and wide-brimmed and sometimes eccentric hats. Shoppers delight in purchasing the latest equestrian styles, and food and drink abound at catered tailgate parties. Jack Russell terriers yelp during their own version of the steeplechase. Crowds gather to watch these dogs race, flying over their own, albeit smaller, fences.

Yet for the riders of the Cup, both the fanfare of the crowds and the dangers of the course are secondary. Their love of horses and the sport keeps these athletes in the race.

opposite In a steeplechase, riders don't just race on flat ground. They also must race through a course of timber and brush fences equally challenging for equestrians and mounts.

below As in many equestrian sports, both men and women may compete as jockeys in a steeplechase. Riders line up evenly at the beginning of the race. Once the flag is dropped, the horses are off. If one horse takes off before the flag falls, riders must line up again to ensure a fair start.

Kelly's Ford

The site of a key Civil War battle in March 1863, Kelly's Ford is approximately sixty miles from Washington, D.C. The Battle of Kelly's Ford, also known as the Battle of Kellysville, was one of the earliest large-scale cavalry engagements in Virginia, where 2,100 Union cavalrymen clashed with 1,000 Confederate cavalrymen. The battle ended in a draw; it was the first time the Confederate cavalry had not won against Union soldiers, which boosted Union confidence and set the stage for later clashes such as Brandy Station and the Gettysburg campaign. Today the former battlefield is a peaceful place where horses graze in green pastures near the waters of the Rappahannock River.

During the Civil War, mounted troops most often were used for reconnaissance, serving as the eyes and ears of generals such as Robert E. Lee and Ulysses S. Grant. Riding a tall, healthy Thoroughbred at Kelly's Ford today, one can imagine the small, well-worn horses that braved the war's exhausting days and nights. Many cavalrymen did not know how to properly care for their equine partners, and while many horses died in battle, many others died from disease, malnourishment, and exhaustion.

At the Inn at Kelly's Ford, all levels of riders can take a guided tour of the battlegrounds, riding where cavalry officers once fought. Wooded trails and open fields make good spots for canters and gallops, and signs along the trail tell the story of the battle. Watch for the spot by the Rappahannock where Confederate Major John Pelham, who earned the nickname "the Gallant Pelham" for his bravery, was fatally wounded.

Guests may stay in the main inn, which dates back to the late 1700s and served as the home of the Kelly family during the Civil War, or the General's Quarters, which dates back to the 1800s. The inn and its outdoor patio overlook the fields and stables. These places allow one to reflect on the lives lost during our nation's struggles and discover American history on horseback.

left About an hour-and-a-half drive from Washington, D.C., riders in Remington, Virginia, travel the path of General Pelham and other brave soldiers who fought and died at the Battle of Kelly's Ford, a historic Civil War battle that was among the earliest large-scale cavalry engagements in the state.

opposite At the Brentsville Courthouse in northern Virginia, members of the Black Horse Troop, a group of dedicated reenactors, meet for drills that are open to the public and offer visitors a chance to observe well-trained horsemen with a keen interest in history.

Middleburg

Middleburg is the unofficial capital of Virginia Hunt Country. This charming village is dotted with brick and stone stores, shops, and restaurants, many with an equestrian theme. White picket fences and stone walls dissect the surrounding area's horse farms, where Olympic hopefuls and well-heeled equestrians stable their mounts. Battlefields remind one of this area's significance during the Civil War, and well-preserved colonial architecture reveals the town's prominence as an eighteenth-century coach stop.

As early as the 1730s, Middleburg was a resting point halfway between Alexandria and Winchester on the Ashby Gap trading route. The town was then known as

Chinn's Crossing, after Joseph Chinn, George Washington's first cousin. Chinn owned a popular tavern and inn for travelers, Chinn's Ordinary, and inherited 3,300 acres in the area. In 1787, Chinn sold 500 acres to Revolutionary War hero Leven Powell, who named the area Middleburg because of its strategic location on the trading route. Strolling Washington, Madison, Jay, Liberty, and Federal Streets, one might give a quiet acknowledgment to Powell, who named these streets with his mind on the new nation's future.

During the Civil War, Confederate Colonel John S. Mosby, who was known as the "Gray Ghost" for his quick and daring raids and escapes, and General

J. E. B. Stuart used Middleburg as a base, and several area buildings served as temporary hospitals. Visitors to Middleburg today can pay tribute to the approximately 1.5 million horses and mules that perished or were injured during the war by stopping by the bronze statue of a Civil War horse outside the National Sporting Library, a research center and library dedicated to horse and field sports that houses rare sporting books. Here visitors can peruse books on angling, falconry, steeplechasing, and sport shooting before viewing rotating art exhibitions.

Since the early 1900s, people have traveled to Middleburg to participate in steeplechases and foxhunts. It was in Middleburg that John F. Kennedy spent weekends during his presidency and Jacqueline Kennedy rode in area hunts. Washington Street, one of the main thoroughfares, caters to such visitors and is lined with equestrian-inspired apparel shops, antique stores, and cozy historic restaurants. Locals start their morning at the Coach Stop restaurant to absorb small-town news and the popular "Horsemen's Special" breakfast. The fieldstone Red Fox Inn still operates much as it did when it was Chinn's Ordinary, welcoming visitors to sleep and dine in an updated eighteenth-century country inn. People are still passing through Middleburg, many to soak in the essence of this quaint area. With history, shops, restaurants, and horse culture, Middleburg is the perfect town for an equestrian escape off horseback.

opposite This bronze statue of a weary Civil War horse that has lost his rider in battle rests outside of the National Sporting Library in Middleburg. The tack and gear that the horse carries are historically accurate.

top Those interested in horses or history or who are just looking to shop a bit find plenty to do along Middleburg's quaint red-brick streets, including breakfasting at the Coach Stop on Washington Street.

above The historic Red Fox Inn welcomes travelers to stay in four-poster beds in a romantic setting. Seven cozy dining rooms offer local wines and signature dishes such as peanut soup.

Chapter 8

Vermont

- Mad River Valley
- Morgan Horse Farm (Middlebury)
- Mountain Top Inn & Resort (Chittenden)

Mad River Valley

In Vermont's Mad River Valley, traditional Vermont can be toured from atop a strong, albeit small, horse on an inn-to-inn ride. At the Icelandic Horse Farm in Fayston, in central Vermont, visitors ride these smooth-gaited, Viking-descended horses through serene country lanes and white birch forests and past cool mountain streams. Nights are spent in cozy country inns, enjoying regional dishes in a bucolic setting.

The drive to the farm winds through wooded roads, past red-and-white barns and old covered bridges. Locals tempt tourists with signs offering maple syrup, cheddar cheese, and other Vermont specialties. At the farm, dozens of Icelandic horses in a variety of colors mill about in paddocks set against a tree-lined mountain. Their shaggy fur and bushy manes protect them from the harsh elements in both Vermont and Iceland. Riders are paired up with seasoned horses for rides of varying length, from a one-day trip to the weeklong inn-to-inn trek. These hardy horses (see the Iceland chapter, page 35) have a special even gait that is ideal for the casual rider, ensuring fewer bumps in the saddle. Though they are on the small side, they are quite strong and able to carry large adults.

On a typical Vermont road lined with shady trees and quaint homes, riders breathe in crisp mountain air as they begin their trek. The Icelandic horses fit the pastoral setting quite well, and their riders enjoy the feeling of floating or gliding as they cross flower-filled meadows and shady mountain trails. A quiet pasture or secret swimming hole may present itself as a good place for a picnic lunch. If the Mad River is not swollen with rain, riders cross it to reach the 1824 House, known for the year it was built, a white-clapboard inn with an attached barn that is listed on the National Historic Register. Here guests stay in charming rooms fitted with elegant antique beds topped with puffy down comforters, perfect for sinking into after a day on the trails.

As riders continue their trek, they arrive at the Mad River Inn, an 1860s Victorian farmhouse with inviting gardens, serene country views, and the mood of a typical Norman Rockwell home, its hardwood floors and picture windows accented by Queen Anne–style furniture. In this rural setting, an appetizer of warm brie, fresh bread, and grapes may be served casually on the back porch. Dinners of grilled salmon, asparagus with hollandaise sauce, portobello mushrooms, rice, and cheesecake topped with raspberries seem quite necessary after burning many calories on the trails.

The gentle Icelandic horses make this an accessible jaunt through central Vermont, and the scenic ride changes with the seasons. In the fall, the leaves evolve into a plethora of brown, red, and orange. Summer brings warm days, a spectrum of green foliage, and sweater-weather nights. The valley's wildflowers are in full bloom come springtime. During the winter, Icelandic horses are in their element, ready to take riders romping through the snow. Cross-country and downhill skiers can alternate between horseback riding and skiing at famous nearby Mad River Glen, and Stowe and Killington are a short drive away.

opposite At the Vermont Icelandic Horse Farm, travelers have a chance to ride Icelandic horses on trips ranging from a half-day excursion to a week-long inn-to-inn voyage.

pages 84–85 Pat and Mikey, Clydesdales at the Mountain Top Inn in central Vermont, are half-brothers. Visitors can learn to tack up and drive these gentle giants. Here Mike Barry, an instructor at the inn, teaches Darley some of the basics.

above Rain or shine, riders venture down quiet country lanes on inn-to-inn rides in Vermont's Mad River Valley. Riders may don protective rain gear, while the Icelandic horses' bushy manes protect them from the elements.

right Riders pass typical Vermont country scenes as they trek through the Mad River Valley. The smooth gait of the Icelandic horse is perfect for casual riders and for enjoying views along the ride.

Mountain Top Inn & Resort

The Mountain Top Inn & Resort is in Chittenden, eleven miles outside the winter ski area of Killington in central Vermont. Nestled in Green Mountain National Forest, which stretches from Quebec to Massachusetts, the inn offers year-round activities, including cross-country skiing and horse-drawn sleigh rides in the winter. Summer lends itself to trail rides, lessons in dressage or cross-country riding, hiking, kayaking, and pontoon boat trips. The Green Mountain trails offer spectacular views and are best explored on foot or aboard a surefooted horse.

The idyllic inn is set above Chittenden Reservoir. Part of its main lodge was a barn in the 1870s, but it didn't house horses—it was used to store turnips grown on the property's farm. In the 1940s, it was converted into a tavern and inn by William Barstow, an associate of Thomas Edison. In the 1950s, President Eisenhower enjoyed the inn and the great area fishing. Today travelers seeking a romantic Vermont inn will feel right at home here.

The stables are just up the lawn from the main inn. A large field of soft grass is an inviting place to warm up with a trot and canter. Wide dirt trails twist past the fishing pond and lesson ring and into the forest. Horses must be fit in order to climb the steep mountain trails, where deer and the occasional moose are spotted. At

a particularly good lookout spot higher up in altitude along the trails, views of the gray-roofed inn and the glassy reservoir are backed by clouds hanging low over nearby hills and Pico Mountain, laced with ski trails. This is an ideal place to picnic or rest before continuing into the forest. After riding, guests enjoy the sunset at a small beach by the reservoir. More active travelers can cut through the still waters in a kayak or pontoon boat, taking in the surrounding tree-covered mountains. Horse lovers who don't ride can visit with Pat and Mikey, the resident Clydesdales, or take a horse-drawn sleigh ride through powdery snow.

The main inn is like a cozy ski lodge, constructed of Douglas fir posts and beams. Fireplaces abound, as do informal sitting areas surrounded by large windows for viewing nature. Suites are decorated with big leather couches accented by equestrian-themed pillows, animal-print wallpaper, fireplaces, and flat-screen televisions. Mixing comfort and luxury, the Mountain Top rooms, chalets, and pet-friendly cabins are ideal for families.

At Highlands Tavern inside the inn, area microbrews are on tap at all times. The dining room offers elegant fare using locally grown Vermont ingredients. Duck glazed with maple syrup and homemade chocolate ice cream are balanced by more healthful options such as green salads sprinkled with fresh berries and crisp seasonal vegetables. Meals are served on china under large antler chandeliers, and diners look out to views of the surrounding mountains. For outdoor-minded horse lovers, the Mountain Top Inn offers a true Vermont escape.

opposite The diverse terrain on the trails surrounding the inn ranges from steep and rocky to flat stretches, superb for trotting and cantering. As in many mountain resort areas, these same trails where horses trod in the summer welcome skiers in the winter.

top The Mountain Top Inn, shown here in full bloom in the summer, welcomes guests with year-round activities, including a robust equestrian program. Its central Vermont location allows for winter cross-country skiing on Green Mountain trails, horse-drawn sleigh rides, and downhill skiing in nearby Killington.

above After riding, visitors can lounge in the dining room or tavern or on the outdoor patio, taking in views of the Green Mountains and Chittenden Reservoir. Green Mountain National Forest extends from Massachusetts to Quebec and offers ample trails for hiking and riding.

Morgan Horse Farm

Outside Middlebury, a beautiful white Victorian-style barn standing out against luxuriant green grass is home to the University of Vermont's Morgan Horse Farm, where top Morgan horses have been bred since the late 1800s. Morgans have been the mounts of presidents, generals, and Vermonters heading west in search of gold and land, and they have played a key role in the development of other breeds. At the university farm, anyone can take a tour to see these beautiful horses up close and perhaps visit with adorable newborn Morgan horses, a special treat.

All Morgan horses can trace their ancestry back to a single bay-colored stallion named Figure, owned by Justin Morgan, a Vermont farmer and composer. Justin Morgan had an interest in horses. His stallion Figure, advertised at stud in New Hampshire and Vermont, served as a source of income for his family. Figure was well suited to frontier life in Vermont. Small but strong, elegant and high-headed, he gained a reputation with the locals, who began to tell stories of the many triumphs of Justin Morgan's horse. Figure was well known for his versatility, too. Whether marching in a parade, pulling out stumps to clear fields, or winning a race, Figure did it with style. It was a tradition to name a horse after its owner in those days, and so Figure became known as "that Justin Morgan horse." He went on to sire horses throughout Vermont that gained a reputation as "horses of all work" for their ability to work long days and steadily cover a lot of rugged New England terrain.

During the Civil War, Morgans were a preferred mount of cavalry officers. They were brave, easy and economical to keep, and said to be loyal to their riders. In the late 1870s, Colonel Joseph Battell began breeding an outstanding group of Morgan horses at his farm, which he turned over to the U.S. government in 1906. Records of his breeding started the American Morgan Register, through which the roots of a Morgan horse's lineage can be traced. The farm continued to operate as a breeding facility, producing Morgans for cavalry officers and others with an interest in the breed, and in

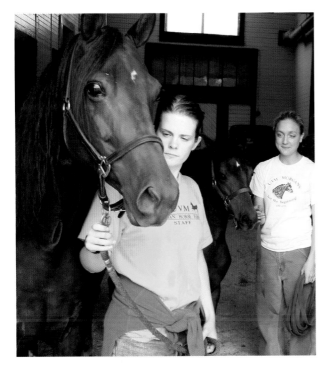

1951 the university took over its ownership and operation. Today the Morgan horse is Vermont's state animal.

Visitors can tour the farm, a National Historic Site, and watch apprentices train the horses in the indoor arena or outside on green grassland. Horses prance around in figure-eight patterns or pull carriages, and there may be award-winning horses in training or foals with their mothers. Up close to these versatile horses, visitors can observe their conformation—graceful arched necks, large, expressive eyes, and compact bodies. Morgan horses come in a variety of colors but are predominantly chestnut, bay, or brown.

Down the road in the small town of Shelburne, travelers can learn more about Morgan horses at the small National Museum of the Morgan Horse, which chronicles the life of Figure and other Morgans throughout history. Visitors can also seek out a local horse show to watch the flash and style of these horses in the ring. Morgan horses are a beloved breed whose legacy remains part of Vermont's and America's history.

opposite Steve Davis, director of Morgan Horse Farm, shows off one of his special Morgans. "I love their temperament. I love their energy," he says. "When I was brought up, my mentor would always ask me, 'Say, Steve, which would you rather have: a horse you have to cluck to, or one you got to say "whoa" to?' I like the one you've got to say 'whoa' to. That [one]'s up on the bit and ready to go."

above Guests can visit the University of Vermont's Morgan Horse Farm, a National Historic Site outside Middlebury, year-round and take a tour led by either Steve or one of the program's apprentices. The farm has four to six apprentices at a time, who spend a year working with the farm's horses.

right From 1907 to 1951, the U.S. government managed the breeding operation at the farm, which was turned over to the University of Vermont in 1951. The U.S. government bred Morgans for the general public and for the cavalry. Morgans have a long history of service to the armed forces, as they were popular mounts during the Civil War.

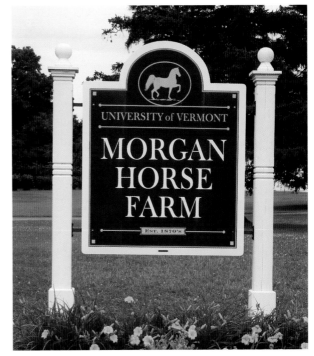

Chapter 9

Colorado

- Northeastern
  Colorado Cattle
  Ranches

San Juan National Forest
- Wilderness Trails Ranch

Northeastern Colorado Cattle Ranches

The blond wheat fields and flat grasslands of northeastern Colorado are vastly different from the Rocky Mountains that so many visualize when they think of the state. This is ranch and farm country where homesteaders settled while gold seekers scoured the mountains. On seven thousand acres at the Colorado Cattle Company, a working cattle ranch, cows roam endless expanses dotted with abandoned buildings and split by small canyons. Visitors do real ranch work, mending fences, branding calves, grooming and saddling horses, and living out their cowboy dreams. The rustic setting of this ranch means only hard workers need apply. Those who venture here take home new skills, and perhaps even a few bumps and bruises, to commemorate their rugged time on the range.

From the ranch, plains that kiss big blue skies stretch out for miles, punctuated by some thousand cows. One can imagine Pony Express riders and pioneers en route to the West Coast crossing this desolate land. At the top of a canyon, an eagle, falcon, or another bird of prey may swoop by out of nowhere. From this high vantage point, the cows below seem tiny, and in the distance an old homestead sits amid the dust of the prairie. Much of this area used to be settled with homes, but harsh conditions, including frequent droughts and dust storms, drove away many settlers. Now much of the land is populated only with corn.

On a cattle drive organized by the ranch, riders travel over a small hill to a watering area to gather the cows. What sounds like an easy task, moving cattle, can be quite difficult, especially if those wily cows don't feel like being relocated. An exuberant border collie may join the ride, bounding down toward the cows, ready for the round-up. The moos get louder as riders surround the cattle. Once the group is in position, cowboys dole out orders and riders focus their attention and energy on moving the herd. Some cows are a little fresher than others, but keeping a slow and steady pace and throwing a feisty cow the evil eye once in a while are a pretty good strategy.

A cattle drive is always an exciting venture, as is learning to rope or to ride a cutting horse. Cutting horses isolate individual animals from a herd. These sheepdog-like horses are quick and agile, and riding one is a roller-coaster jaunt for the novice. After a day aboard a spirited cutting horse, visitors to the ranch are served an informal meal and cozy down in tidy log cabins before tomorrow's work begins. There are lots of adventures to be had on a working cattle ranch, and energetic travelers who are ready to work will have quite a ride.

opposite Cattle surround water tanks as wranglers tell guests where to take their positions for the cattle drive. In this part of Colorado, the land can be dry and dusty; along with impending storms, this can mean cattle must be driven to new pastures.

above Darley learns to "get loose" on a cutting horse during a clinic at the Colorado Cattle Company. Good balance is essential when riding these high-performance horses.

pages 92–93 Pass Creek Trail leads to the base of Engineer Mountain, which thrusts skyward amid ominous clouds. For riders and horses, this trail can be challenging.

San Juan National Forest

Consisting of several peaks reaching fourteen thousand feet, vertical canyons, and extreme switchbacks, the San Juan National Forest offers challenging trails, yet riders and horses who explore this part of southwestern Colorado will be greatly rewarded by its breathtaking scenery. Although most San Juan trails are interesting, the ride up Pass Creek Trail to the base of Engineer Mountain is exceptionally dramatic.

Gradually winding through a subalpine forest to higher altitudes, riders gaze up in clearings at Engineer Mountain towering above, its green-and-red-hued slopes leaping skyward as the ultimate climb. Here, in the quiet shade by a pond, the air is already growing cooler.

Farther up, it will grow cold. As riders conquer switchbacks, the rocky trails narrow and the soil alongside falls away to steep wooded inclines.

Above timberline, fields of wildflowers—primrose, geranium, Indian paintbrush, and orchids—are colonized by hummingbirds. In July and August, the weather is as warm as it gets here, and the wildflowers are in full bloom. Still, riders may face snowdrifts, since these trails run across the north face of the mountain. August is monsoon season, bringing rain and possibly hail. As the altitude increases, so does the volatility of the weather. Gray cumulus clouds may stack up against one side of the mountain and then pass overhead in a fit of sleet.

From around twelve thousand feet, at the base of Engineer Mountain, Lake Electra can be seen shimmering in the distance. At what seems like the top of the world, views of the awe-inspiring Rocky Mountains overwhelm the senses. On a clear day, vistas extend all the way to New Mexico.

Other options for horse trails up the mountain include Engineer Mountain Trail, which is a little rougher than Pass Creek, or Engine Creek, which extends into the general area. Riders in San Juan National Forest may bring their own horses or head out with an experienced outfitter such as Anne Rapp of Rapp Corral in Durango. For those bringing their own horses, the Lower Hermosa Campground is approximately eighteen miles away from Engineer Mountain. But no matter how one rides here, it's a journey not to be missed. The natural beauty of the San Juan Mountains can only be described as awesome.

Off the trail, many old mines dot the mountains, some of them yet to be documented. One can experience the history of the mining days by riding the nearby historic Durango & Silverton Narrow Gauge Railroad. The railroad, which has been running for over 125 years, was built to transport precious metals from the mining town of Silverton through Durango and onward. As soon as the scenic beauty of the route was discovered, guests began to ride the train, too. The ride from Durango to Silverton and back is a real adventure—the wheels rattle and the steam engine whistles as the train climbs three thousand feet along the Animas River.

The well-preserved old mining town of Silverton is a National Historic Landmark. Greene Street is its main thoroughfare, with shops, restaurants, and historic inns, but Blair Street may be the most interesting one. At the height of Silverton's mining days, Blair Street held more than thirty saloons, gambling houses, and brothels in a three-block stretch. It's a bit quieter today, but one can imagine what life was like in this classic Western boomtown on a stroll through its colorful streets.

above Diverse mountain scenery and demanding trails await the rider in San Juan National Forest. As paths wind to higher altitudes, the air grows colder and the trees begin to disappear.

opposite Lake Electra shimmers in the distance as Anne Rapp and Darley continue farther into the high country. On a clear day from this vantage point, one can spot New Mexico.

pages 98–99 Guide Anne Rapp's horses take a break. "This is a huge chunk of forest that we're in here. In the San Juan National Forrest alone you could ride for years, I think, and still love everything," says Anne.

Wilderness Trails Ranch

Forty minutes northeast of Durango in southwestern Colorado, Wilderness Trails Ranch is in a valley surrounded by the San Juan Mountains. This family-run ranch sits in the state's largest roadless area and presents many options for exploring on horseback, offering both top-notch riding on well-trained trail horses and lessons for those who haven't spent a lot of time in the saddle. Many visitors are families with children who will take their first rides here at the ranch. And with a Le Cordon Bleu–trained executive chef, there are always scrumptious fixin's after a day on the trails.

Wilderness Trails borders the Weminuche and Piedra wilderness areas. The Weminuche, the largest wilderness area in Colorado, takes its name from the Ute Indian tribe, who once lived and hunted here. The Piedra area consists of more than sixty thousand acres of meadows, canyons, and forests. Trails lead out from the ranch through aspen groves to open meadows that are ideal for fast riding. In July and August, these meadows burst with colorful wildflowers. On a slow pass along a meadow trail, riders may spot a coyote or brown or black bear sheltering in the tall grass.

Trails wind to a lookout point over Vallecito Reservoir (*vallecito* is Spanish for "little valley"), which sits at eight thousand feet in a high alpine valley surrounded by towering granite and wooded peaks. The Los Pinos, or the Pine River, flows into the reservoir through the western portion of the Weminuche Wilderness. At the lookout point, riders are surrounded by the skeletal remains of trees burned during a 2002 fire that nearly devastated Wilderness Trails Ranch; the charred areas are a reminder of the fragile local environment. Serene views of Vallecito's calm waters beckon below, and riders may spot a relative or friend water skiing or fishing.

Back at the ranch, guests feast on healthful meals such as chicken with spicy green-chile sauce, rice, beans, grilled vegetables, and homemade cake with fresh berries. Nights may be spent learning to line dance or enjoying s'mores by an outdoor fire. When not on the trails, guest may work with cattle, driving them from the hills down to the ranch or to new grazing areas. Staying at this southern Colorado ranch allows one to explore a vast wilderness by day and hunker down in a warm cabin at night.

opposite Trails wind through forests of aspen in the Piedra Wilderness. At Wilderness Trails Ranch, all levels of riders, including children, are welcome on riding adventures in the largest roadless area in Colorado.

top Gene Roberts, who has owned Wilderness Trails with his wife, Jan, since 1970, tells guests his philosophy of riding and working with horses during a guest orientation session. Gene and Jan are both certified riding instructors who work to ensure guests enjoy safe and fun riding vacations.

above Guests saddle up at Cowboy's Place, the rustic brown barn near the cabins and main lodge. Here riders are split into groups based on their level of experience and head out for trail rides, cattle work, or a wilderness trout-fishing ride.

Chapter 10

Wyoming

• Wild Mustangs
   (McCullough Peaks)
• Shoshone National Forest
Jackson Hole • • T Cross Ranch (Dubois)

T Cross Ranch

Riding out among gray-green sagebrush and wheat-colored grass in the Wyoming countryside with the glacier-capped Wind River Mountains in the distance, one feels at peace with the world. Cut off from the trappings of modern society, T Cross Ranch, outside the small western town of Dubois and two hours east of Jackson Hole, is an authentic dude ranch. Guests trade in their suits and cars for jeans and horses at this early-twentieth-century ranch, if only for a week; relaxing in a rocking chair on the front porch of a quiet cabin after a day's riding, then sitting down to a homemade meal, they experience the satisfaction of a full day well spent. The essence of T Cross is that of the homesteaders who once graced these lands with their pioneer spirit.

It is thought that in the 1890s a cattle rancher named Ernest Hadden officially settled the 160 acres of land where T Cross now rests. Henry Seipt, a German immigrant and veteran of the Spanish-American War, took over the ranch in 1918 and named it the Hermitage.

During the 1920s and '30s, when dude ranches began to gain popularity across the American West, Seipt welcomed guests. For these East Coast "dudes," ranches were romantic destinations that offered adventures in wide-open spaces and the chance to play cowboy.

In 1929, Helen and Bob Cox purchased the Hermitage and opened their newly expanded and newly named T Cross Ranch to guests. Its pine cabins with wood-beamed ceilings, fireplaces, and log furniture are still illuminated by natural light. The fourth-generation ranching family that runs T Cross now, the Cardalls, use only original materials when replacing and repairing broken fixtures, such as wooden door latches and bed frames. This kind of attention to detail takes a lot of work, but the extra care allows T Cross to preserve its historic structures.

Generations of families have visited T Cross. A tradition started by wealthy Easterners in the 1930s now includes guests from all over the world. While some ranches have fought extinction by broadening

their appeal with modern amenities such as luxury spas, T Cross has remained faithfully and historically Western. It is surrounded by Shoshone National Forest and backs up to the largest roadless area in the lower forty-eight states, making for lots of space to explore. Riders can climb over twelve thousand feet into the mountains to take in spectacular views of surrounding cliffs and mountains or to catch brook trout, rainbow trout, or mountain whitefish in the shallow waters of Horse Creek.

Other visitors, those seeking history rather than a well-stocked stream, drive the long, unpaved road to the town of Dubois, along the Wind River. Dubois is on an old trapper route: American frontiersmen Kit Carson and Jim Bridger passed through the town in the 1800s, and notorious outlaw Butch Cassidy later followed. Ranches such as T Cross help safeguard and conserve land and nature, so that riders can quench their curiosity about the past while getting away from the unending demands of modern life.

top "People who come to dude ranches have a curiosity about what was," says Ken Neal, who recently retired from running T Cross. "Fortunately, we still have some area left that shows what it was like prior to the arrival of modern civilization. We think it's certainly special."

opposite Mark Cardall, who runs T Cross Ranch with his wife, Gretchen, leads riders to Horse Creek, a great spot for fly-fishing only steps away from the ranch cabins.

above T Cross's pine cabins offer wooden rocking chairs on shaded porches. Guests may sit and read a book or watch horses in pastures backed by the Absaroka Mountains. In the historic lodge, pictured here, guests gather for hearty ranch food. The lodge was built by hand in the 1930s.

pages 102–103 Tara Flaherty, Darley Newman, and Tuff Flaherty (back to front) navigate down a steep, rocky incline in Shoshone National Forest. Tuff advises riders to "let the horse pick his own path going through the rocks. Leave just a little bit of extra rein, so that he knows that he can go ahead and do as he wants."

Shoshone National Forest

U XU Ranch is between the town of Cody and the eastern entrance of Yellowstone National Park, resting along the North Fork of the Shoshone River in an area Teddy Roosevelt called the most scenic fifty-two miles in America. Visitors to the ranch play the part of renegade cowboys, riding in the vast Shoshone National Forest surrounded by the Absaroka Mountain Range.

UXU Ranch has welcomed guests since 1929, housing them in rustic refurbished log cabins, including the Hideout Cabin, which dates back to 1892. Dinner is served in the dining room or outside on the porch, where guests can drink wine under the stars and watch horses graze in the pastures while devouring elk, melt-in-your-mouth muffins, organic vegetables, Parmesan risotto, and other hearty dishes. On trail rides, hot lunches by a campfire may include grilled kebabs, couscous, and grilled-cheese sandwiches. This family-friendly ranch attracts travelers seeking adventurous and diverse riding vacations.

Horses and riders wade through the cool, swiftly flowing North Fork, a prime spot for fly-fishing, on what the wranglers call the Spectacular Ride. This ride climbs approximately two thousand feet on steep mountain trails to the top of a high ridge. On the final climb, the terrain is steep, and there are no resting points for the horses, so riders must keep them going straight up. Those afraid of riding on narrow trails that drop off into deep canyons may not appreciate this ride, but for those who are up to the challenge, the panoramic views at the top are well worth it. From the clouds, the ranch below looks like a speck, and snow-capped mountain-tops glimmer in the distance.

Memories abound of the explorers and adventurers who traveled through these parts, including John Colter, a member of the Lewis and Clark expedition; Jim Bridger, a mountain man and trapper; and the native Shoshone Indians. Shoshone National Forest is named for the tribe, which once used the area as a hunting ground. Other tribes, such as the Nez Perce, Northern Cheyenne, Sioux, and Arapahoe, also hunted and traveled here. The forest is vast, encompassing almost two and a half million acres, with elevations ranging from 4,600 to over 13,000 feet. As riders pass through meadows of wildflowers, they'll spot sand-colored, finger-shaped rock formations, called hoodoos, projecting into the air. The Shoshone and other Native American tribes believed that hoodoos were the home of powerful spirits, and visitors today can still sense their mystery.

opposite Tuff Flaherty, owner of UXU Ranch, rides into the North Fork of the Shoshone River. Surrounded by the Absaroka Mountain Range, the ranch offers challenging riding in Shoshone National Forest.

left Ray Flaherty, Tuff's father, rests during a picnic ride. Lunch on the trails is gourmet, and cooked over an open fire.

top Fly-fishing guide Wilson Stark tacks up his horse at UXU Ranch. The ranch is on the North Fork of the Shoshone River, where there are ample opportunities to go fly-fishing, and offers many side trips, including a day trip to Yellowstone National Park, for non-riders and those who want a break from the saddle.

above Riders pass beneath rock formations known as hoodoos, which the Shoshone and other Native Americans believed housed powerful spirits.

Jackson Hole

About twenty minutes from downtown Jackson Hole, travelers can take off into the wilderness of Bridger-Teton National Forest on a pack trip, on which riders bundle their gear onto packhorses and camp out overnight in the wild. Pack trips can be challenging and strenuous, especially for novices, as riders may spend many hours in the saddle. But riders are rewarded by their horseback venture into nature: they probably won't see another human or automobile along the way. Those with an interest in history will delight in exploring the untamed wilderness, much as history's famous mountainmen would have during the early 1800s when Jackson Hole was a lively intersection for the fur trade. Jim Bridger (the park's namesake) and Kit Carson, frontiersmen and trappers, were two of the legendary figures who journeyed through this area.

Bridger-Teton National Forest encompasses more than 3.4 million acres in western Wyoming. Trails wind through alpine meadows, fields of wildflowers, and forests of aspen, Douglas fir, and Engelmann spruce. Mountains, including the majestic Grand Tetons, tower in the distance, and around every corner the forest yields something new. Wyoming's state flower, the red Indian paintbrush, brightens up the trails, as if strategically placed to garner attention. Though beautiful, these flowers act as parasites,

feeding on the roots of other plants. Meadows may hold the remnants of an old homesteader's cabin or offer sweeping views of mountainsides.

Many tour companies offer pack trips around Jackson Hole. Jackson Hole Horse Pack and Fishing Trips offer visitors the flexibility of choosing a one-night or longer pack trip into Bridger-Teton National Forest, where guests stay at their Willow Creek campsite, nestled in the seclusion of a forest. Spacious white canvas tents fitted with cots and mattresses allow guests to rough it in relative comfort. But pack trips vary in their accommodations. While some offer hot showers, others may send guests to the nearest clear mountain stream to bathe in cool waters. Stargazers can stay warm by a campfire as the big Wyoming sky fills with a million stars, and days are spent riding the array of trails that branch out from camp. Saddlesore travelers can fly-fish for native trout or hike. The trips sound simple, but the calm they offer is very attractive for those looking to unwind.

below Pack trips allow riders to get away from the bustle of daily life, venture to remote destinations and view the land at a relaxed pace. The sun sets on the Wyoming trails, as riders head home.

opposite An area about the size of the state of Connecticut, Bridger-Teton National Forest comes alive in the summer months with colorful flowers and wildlife. Trails wind through a meadow in Bridger-Teton National Forest.

Wild Mustangs

The McCullough Peaks, about twenty-two miles outside Cody, are home to a herd of wild horses whose story is intertwined with the history of the West. In this approximately 110,000-acre area of flatland, rolling foothills, steep cliffs, and rugged canyons, horses with buckskin, strawberry roan, bay, chestnut, and sorrel coats stand out amid the brown, red, and sage desert badlands.

On a horseback tour of the area, visitors can spend time with War Bonnet, Grey Face, Raven, and other wild horses that local Kenny Martin knows so well. At McCullough Peaks, Kenny leads visitors on tours (booked through Red Canyon Wild Mustang Tours)

to the best places to spot Mustangs. Looking for fresh piles of manure is one way to gauge recent horse activity in the area, but there are certain favorite grazing areas to check first. The horses at McCullough Peaks appear strong and healthy, despite the harsh conditions here—the eroded soil in the badlands is rich in clay and sparse in vegetation.

The Mustangs travel in bands that usually consist of a stallion, several mares, and their offspring. A mare leads the band to search for food and water. The stallion protects the mares and their young from danger and tries to attract new mares and produce new foals. Bachelor stallions try to steal mares from other bands, which

causes the band's stallion to snort and posture to show his dominance. This may be enough; if not, the stallions rise on their hind legs and fight.

The horses at McCullough Peaks are thought to be the descendants of Spanish horses brought to North America in the 1500s. They may also be descendants of horses used in Buffalo Bill's Wild West Show. Buffalo Bill, whose real name was William Frederick Cody, was a frontiersman, soldier, and colorful character. His live touring extravaganza, based on his adventures in the West, began in 1883 and ran for three decades. It featured a cast of hundreds acting out various Western scenes such as Custer's Last Stand, the Pony Express, and train robberies. The performers wore extravagant costumes and toured like rock stars. Their horses traveled with them, and together they fueled adventurous and romantic fantasies of the American West. Locals say that when the show was not touring, its horses were allowed to graze at McCullough Peaks. Some may not have been rounded up or were simply left to form the herds that inhabit this dramatic area today.

Antelope, deer, and mountain lions roam McCullough Peaks, too, though they are not as easy to spot as the horses. Bill Cody's namesake town, which he helped found in 1895, is just down the road. Here visitors can take in more history at the Buffalo Bill Historical Center, attend a night rodeo, or just stroll through the shops. But McCullough Peaks and the Mustangs that roam its wild spaces—and its visitors, with their binoculars and backpacks—keep the pulse of the Old West beating.

opposite A foal walks alongside members of its band at McCullough Peaks, just outside Cody. These horses are Mustangs, wild horses that are the descendants of the horses brought to North America by Spanish explorers.

left The Wild Free-Roaming Horses and Burros Act of 1971 protects wild horses and burros that roam on public land, as at McCullough Peaks. The Act named horses "living symbols of the historic and pioneer spirit of the West."

above In the 1950s, Velma Johnston, a Nevada resident known as "Wild Horse Annie," worked to protect horses like this large black stallion. Velma was outraged at the often inhumane way horses were captured on America's rangelands. Her grassroots efforts made the treatment of feral horses a public issue and led to the passage of a 1959 law that prohibited the use of motorized vehicles to hunt wild horses on public land.

Chapter 11

California Wine Country

Redwoods(Armstrong Redwoods
State Reserve)

- Sugarloaf Ridge State Park
- Sonoma Vineyards

Sonoma Vineyards

Some have compared California wine country, with its abundant vineyards, gourmet food, and laid-back vibe, to Tuscany or the south of France. Among the best—and most unusual—ways to experience the area is to tour it on horseback. Instead of simply heading into a winery, tasting a few varietals, and then departing, visitors at Larson Family Winery in Sonoma can saddle up to explore a vineyard, much as the early California and European vintners did. This mode of travel both grants a behind-the-scenes look at winery life and is a romantic thoroughfare through California wine country.

Larson Family Winery is a small family-run vineyard a short drive from Sonoma's historic Spanish pueblo-style plaza, which is surrounded by wine and cheese shops, bakeries, eccentric gift stores, and historic buildings. On its northeast corner, the old Sonoma Mission dates back to 1823. This was the last and northernmost of the twenty-one California missions to be founded. Before the mission fathers arrived, the area was inhabited by native tribes (Pomo, Miwok, and Wappo Tribes). Mexican General Mariano Guadalupe Vallejo took over the mission in 1834 and helped settlers grow crops and grapes on the fertile land. Later, California briefly became a sovereign nation, but quickly joined the United States. After San Francisco's great earthquake and fire of 1906, many urbanites flocked to the Sonoma area and became chicken farmers. This farming legacy may seem a far cry from today's wine shops and chic country restaurants, but the small town of Sonoma still holds fast to its agricultural roots, turning away from mass development in favor of intimacy and small-town flavor.

Larson Family Winery is part of Sonoma's historic legacy. The vineyard's grounds by Sonoma Creek once served as a landing where travelers from San Francisco Bay docked their vessels to explore Sonoma. Boats from San Francisco also brought European visitors to this area, perhaps as early as the 1820s. In 1899, Michael Millerick, great-grandfather of the winery's current owner, Tom Larson, purchased and settled 101 acres of the property and its old steamboat captain's house. Millerick was a cutting-horse champion, and from 1929 until the 1950s, the Millerick ranch was proud to host the Sonoma Rodeo, which drew crowds of thousands, including well-known cowboys of the time. Black-and-white photos and other equestrian memorabilia inside the winery attest to this colorful history.

A tractor could roll by as riders begin down a row of chardonnay vines. They can reach out and pick grapes right off the vines as they slowly meander through trellised rows dripping with green fruit. The Carneros region's manicured hills rise in the distance. This area's cool climate, combined with the fog and breezy moderate temperatures produced by San Francisco Bay and the nearby Pacific Ocean, is ideal for growing chardonnay and pinot noir grapes.

After riding, visitors may relax at a Larson family barbecue, eating roast beef much as spectators at the Sonoma Rodeo did in the 1930s. Between glasses of wine and grilled treats, visitors may opt to play a game of bocce or simply to gaze at a field of sunlit vines. Where livestock used to roam, a redwood barn now holds oak barrels and a comfortable tasting room. Guests may sample a 2003 cabernet sauvignon, winner at the California State Fair, and pair bits of chocolate with a cherry-flavored merlot. It's these gourmet delicacies and the equally rich history of horses on this land that make riding at Larson Family Winery a real Sonoma treat.

opposite Darley and Rafael Hernandez laugh as they ride through the grounds of the Larson Family Winery in Sonoma. Through his Wine Country Trail Rides, Rafael leads riders on close-up tours of the vineyard.

pages 112–113 In Sugarloaf Ridge State Park, Erin Ellis, who grew up riding in the park, lets riders in on her favorite part, when "the wind comes up and you look around and the whole ride gets quiet and everyone, including my horse Deuce, just listens."

right Horses have a long legacy on the vineyard's grounds, which were the site of the old Sonoma Rodeo. Riders can also tour the winery land in a horse-drawn cart pulled by Huey and Duey or enter the winery to see equestrian photographs and memorabilia on the tasting room's walls.

Redwoods

In the Russian River region outside the town of Guerneville, about an hour and a half north of San Francisco, riders can venture into a redwood grove at Armstrong Redwoods State Reserve. The park was named after Colonel James Armstrong, a lumberman who in the 1870s sought to preserve its primeval forest from logging operations. The tallest trees in the world—in fact, the tallest living things on earth—redwoods can reach over 350 feet, about the length of a football field. These giant trees covered a wider swath of this area before nineteenth-century logging began.

Armstrong Redwoods Pack Station leads riders on nature tours through these imposing giants on well-trained quarter horses. This versatile breed possesses a calm disposition that makes it ideal on the forest's shady trails. Riding through large stumps that have been sliced in two to accommodate hikers and riders, one can marvel at the numerous rings that reveal the trees' age. The width of these trees can dwarf both horses and hikers. Even though some of these trees became stumps in the mid-1800s, many have not decomposed. Coastal redwoods are amazingly resilient, with thick bark and high levels of tannin that make them naturally resistant to insects and fire. Redwoods need moisture to survive, and the thick fog that surrounds these trees in the summer, coupled with

winter rains, is vital to their growth. A belt of redwoods extends from southern Oregon to central California, some of the trees are more than 2,000 years old. In Armstrong Redwoods State Reserve, the oldest tree is more than 1,400 years old and the tallest is 310 feet high.

Uprooted trees reveal the shallow root system that can extend over one hundred feet from the trees' base and intermingle with the roots of other redwoods, helping to keep these tall trees stable. Riders also may pass a "goosepen," a natural pen created when fire guts a redwood trunk. Early settlers took advantage of these enclosures by housing their geese, chickens, and ducks inside them. Today the woods are quiet, except for the occasional deer, squirrel, and bird wandering among the dripping needles of the Douglas fir and the leaves of the fragrant California bay laurel.

The park's dynamic ecosystem changes along with the seasons. Spring brings the pink blossoms of the woodrose shrub, delicate white fairybells, and a green carpet of redwood sorrel. Wintertime means mushrooms, moss, and green braken ferns that turn the floor into a fuzzy blanket, and rains that cause creeks to swell and move swiftly. Throughout the year, the light constantly changes. As the sun moves across the sky, different parts of the forest become illuminated: a small creek where a tiny bird stops for a drink; a knobby burl on a redwood's bark; a squirrel searching for food. Riding among these giant trees, where other travelers have journeyed for more than a thousand years, is humbling.

left In Armstrong Redwoods State Reserve, the oldest tree is more than 1,400 years old and the tallest is 310 feet high.

opposite Darley and Laura Ayers, who with her husband runs Armstrong Redwoods Pack Station, pass a large stump, whose size compared to the horses lends perspective to these living giants.

Sugarloaf Ridge State Park

At the headwaters of Sonoma Creek, trails lined with oak and redwood trees, giant ferns, and soft mountain grass meander through classic Sonoma scenery. Here at Sugarloaf Ridge State Park, twenty-five miles of trails lead riders through golden hills. Triple Creek Horse Outfit guides riders through the park on sunset, picnic lunch, and full-moon rides. On trips to the park's Vista Point, riders can watch as sundown blends pinks, blues, and reds across the Napa and Sonoma valleys, or they can ride meadow trails along Sugarloaf Ridge, bounded only by blue skies and the occasional hawk.

The ridge is named after the jagged pieces of sugar that people bought before the turn of the twentieth century. When a customer purchased sugar, it was broken off a conical loaf, and these uneven pieces resemble the top of Sugarloaf Ridge. The Wappo Indians, who once lived in villages along the creek, hunted and gathered in the park's woods. Though the Wappos resisted the Spaniards who settled in the area, their tribe was swiftly decimated by cholera and smallpox. Later, other settlers homesteaded in the area, and remnants of their homes still can be seen today.

Here in the Mayacamas Mountains, the landscape changes with the elevation. On the summit of Bald Mountain, clear days offer views of the Sierra Nevada and San Francisco Bay. Riders watch for blacktail deer, bobcats, raccoons, and foxes as the trail winds over a bridge crossing Sonoma Creek. Outcroppings of the red and orange shaggy madrone, a tree that sheds its papery bark, stand out amid shaded forest trails. California laurel, oak, and gray pine rise amid the graceful dark red limbs of manzanitas and the gray-green leaves of coyote bush. Because of their twisted, unusual branches, manzanita trees appear as if they have been shaped by ocean waves and are thus nicknamed "mountain driftwood." Riders are glad for their well-conditioned horses as the trails grow increasingly steep, and enjoy the freshening air as they rise out of the forest toward Vista Point and take in unfolding views of the Napa and Sonoma valleys. In the middle of wine country, the land and its abundant gifts offer a sense of peace and prosperity.

opposite Erin Ellis, who guides riders with her company Triple Creek Horse Outfit, and Darley pass through fields of grass in Sugarloaf Ridge State Park.

right Riders who join Erin gain a unique look at the park and nature. "I like to give our guests history," says Erin. "But I also like there to be quiet time . . . to hear the birds—to hear the wind. Things that, especially for people living in the city, you don't experience. Things that you just can't find in everyday life sometimes."

Chapter 12

Maui

- Makawao and
  Piiholo Ranch

- Haleakala
  Kipahulu

Haleakala

Haleakala National Park in eastern Maui is home to Haleakala, an active shield volcano with one of the most surreal terrains on earth. Traveling from Maui's beaches to the summit, visitors wind along a meandering thirty-seven-mile road, catching stellar views of the coastline and bright, blue Pacific as they climb through dense clouds to over ten thousand feet past the farms of Maui's horse country. Once at the top, looking into the volcano's abyss of jagged red, brown, purple, and green peaks and powdery mounds of cinder, one finds it hard to believe that people ride twenty-five hundred feet down into this crater. But for those up to the challenge, horseback riding is one of the best ways to see Haleakala and get a sense of how Maui and the rest of Earth's land were formed.

Though Haleakala is an active volcano, it is not currently erupting. Its last eruption is thought to have occurred in 1790, not so long ago, geologically speaking. At some point, another is due.

The horses that undertake the journey to the crater floor on the Sliding Sands Trail, descending from around ten thousand feet to approximately seventy-five hundred feet, have to be fit and adventurous, as do the riders. Descending into the crater means adjusting to a dramatic change in altitude. The weather, too, can change dramatically. Clouds roll in and out, covering the entire bowl in a sheet. Riders may be lost in a sea of clouds, unable to see beyond their horses' heads. This eerie occurrence may dissipate quickly as the sun shines down, clearing the clouds and revealing the gigantic space that is the crater.

Haleakala means "house of the sun." During the day, as the sun changes position in the sky, the colors of Haleakala's terrain shift in response. Some say sunset is the most spectacular time, but each hour of the day reveals new shades. Various vantage points along the Sliding Sands Trail disclose large cinder cones on the crater floor and the dark rivers of lava flows from years past. The cinder cones include reddish-black and rust-colored Pu'u o Maui, which at approximately five-hundred-feet tall is the largest cinder cone in the crater. Gauging its precise height is difficult, however. In the crater, distances are deceiving. The entire island of Manhattan would fit inside the crater, but there are no points of reference to provide a sense of perspective.

As riders descend through switchbacks, the temperature grows increasingly cooler. Brown and red cinders slide and crunch beneath horses' hooves. The Haleakala area, which looks so barren, actually is home to many rare insects and its own particular ecosystem, which makes keeping to the trails important. Riders discover hearty plants that have been able to survive hot days, freezing nights, and little rain in this desolate environment, including the rare and stunning Haleakala silversword, found nowhere else on Earth. This spiky silver plant's skin and hairs reflect the sun's rays and protect it from freezing temperatures inside the crater. It can take up to fifty years for the silversword to bloom—producing hundreds of delicate purple flowers that rise from a stalk that can grow up to six feet tall—and after it does, it dies. The best time to see the bloom is June and July, when the plants stand out amid the rusty-red Haleakala cinders.

Exploring Haleakala, it's easy to understand why ancient Hawaiians believed this crater to be sacred. Late-afternoon visitors have been known to experience the Specter of Broken, a phenomenon in which one's shadow on the clouds is encircled by a rainbow. In this unusual setting, spectacular things do happen.

opposite Riders must navigate a few rocky places on the trails. Doug Smith of Pony Express Tours, who has been leading riders into Haleakala Crater for over twenty-five years, leads Darley through a more challenging section of the Sliding Sands Trail.

pages 120–121 Large cinder cones rise from the valley floor. These mounds of ash and rocks formed when eruptions fountained from volcanic vents.

right top As the sun moves across the sky during the day, different parts of the crater are illuminated. As many times as Doug has ridden into Haleakala over the past twenty-five years, he still says, "There'll always be one day you'll see something you've never seen." Even though riders take the same trail in and out, its shifting appearance makes some swear they're on a new trail on the way home.

right bottom The Haleakala silversword, found only here in the crater, shines in the sun. This silver plant blooms once and then dies, making June and July sightings of its fragile purple flowers a special treat for riders.

Kipahulu

To get to this remote section of Maui, visitors must brave the Road to Hana, a winding scenic highway that runs along the northeastern coast. With more than six hundred curves and many one-lane bridges, the sixty-eight-mile drive to Kipahulu takes at least three hours. Along the way, there are many tempting places to stop to see waterfalls, rainforests, and awesome coastal cliff views. This lush tropical area is home to Oheo Gulch, popularly known as the Seven Sacred Pools, where there are dozens of waterfalls and swimming holes. Stands selling fresh fruit, handmade jewelry, and tropical flowers line the road. You won't see a chain shop here, just locally owned and run venues with regional products. This is charming old Hawaii at its best.

Maui Stables is run by natives of Kipahulu whose ancestors have lived in this region for hundreds of years. Living here has meant learning to survive off the land, and elders have passed down their way of life from generation to generation. Each morning, the stables' *alaka'i*, or guides, gather to say an *oli*, or chant, learned from their elders. Riders are asked to participate before they mount up.

By the stables, Kipahulu's main road is lined with farms, homes, and a multitude of edible plants and fruits. Guides pick snacks for guest riders, including

exotic apple bananas, papaya, and breadfruit, a staple Hawaiian starch. Fruits, fresh fish from the sea, and medicinal plants from the forest give people here a bountiful subsistence.

Old rock walls line the main road in Kipahulu. Beyond them are sacred temples and distinct districts that shed light on the Hawaiian way of life before contact with the Western world. The Hawaiians had laws called the *kapu* ("taboo" or "forbidden") system, which dictated what was allowed and what was not. Chiefs enforced the laws, which regulated such matters as what fish could be caught when. In a society dependent on nature's gifts for survival, the *kapu* system helped ensure that residents were in balance with nature and one another.

Off the road in the rainforest, rocky trails climb to higher elevations past bamboo, ferns, feral cows, fruit trees, and lush vegetation. This area is part of Haleakala National Park, but is very different from the volcanic terrain of the crater. It's humid, wet, and green here and teeming with many endangered birds. Near the end of the ride, Waimoku Falls, the tallest waterfalls on Maui, rise four hundred feet, backed by lava rocks and abundant vegetation in this pristine, culturally rich area.

opposite Keoni Smith, a guide at Maui Stables, prepares an on-the-trail snack as Darley munches on ripe papaya picked right off a tree on a trek to Waimoku Falls in Haleakala National Park. When papaya is green, it can be boiled and tastes like squash, but when it is ripe, it can be enjoyed straight from the branch.

top Horses navigate through high grass in the rainforest. Vehicles are banned in this part of the forest, so traveling on surefooted horses is a great way to explore the jungle's higher reaches.

above This part of the island is known for its lush terrain and many waterfalls. Riders may decide to take a dip after riding. Many falls are accessible along the Road to Hana; others, like tall Waimoku Falls, can be seen on a ride with Maui Stables.

Makawao and Piiholo Ranch

Maui's Upcountry is cowboy country. On the slopes of Mount Haleakala, ranches abound. The air is a little cooler, and what the locals call Maui mist makes for frequent rainbows. Upcountry is home to ranchers and horsemen, as well as an influx of artists and locally owned restaurants. It is also the home to ranches such as Piiholo that welcome visitors for exploration on horseback.

The cowboy enclave of Makawao is the main town Upcountry. Its storefronts haven't changed much since the mid-nineteenth century, but the vibe here is a mix of Old West and New Age. Baldwin Avenue, the main drag, houses Western clothing shops, artists' studios, hitching posts, and yoga and wellness centers. Less than five square miles in area, this town bustles in spring and summer with rodeos, including a grand Fourth of July rodeo and parade.

Just up the road, six generations of the Baldwin family have ranched on Maui for over one hundred years. Their Piiholo Ranch invites guests to experience the Upcountry on horseback. Riders saddle up with one of the Baldwins or a guide to tour this working cattle ranch. Most visitors ride a quarter horse, a versatile American breed used on many ranches throughout the United States.

Piiholo Ranch is on the edge of the rainforest, so a diverse number of plants and birds make their home here. As riders pass along shady trails, the scent of the eucalyptus forest mingles with the fragrant yellow flowers of ginger trees. Past the 450-foot drop into Maliko Gulch, through a stream, and up a small hill, cows graze the ranch's open pastures, which offer panoramic views of the Pacific Ocean. Nearby, riders can observe the endangered nene, Hawaii's state bird. This goose, which looks like a Canada goose, is named after the soft *nay-nay* sound that it makes when it eats. All these sounds, scents, and sights of Maui's Upcountry are best noticed from the quiet back of a horse.

top Trails lead through a towering eucalyptus forest toward Maliko Gulch. Rides trek through forests to lush pastures dotted with cows overlooking the ocean.

above On a trail ride, guests can check cattle in pastures backed by the brilliant Pacific Ocean. The ranch raises big-horned Corriente cattle, whose athletic, lean bodies make them ideal for rodeo events.

opposite Riders pick up the pace to beat impending rains. Maui mist moves in and out quickly here, settling the dusty trails and cooling off horses and riders.

Chapter 13

Hawaii's Big Island

- Kahua Ranch
- The Valley of the Kings
  (Waipi'o)

Parker Ranch

Parker Ranch

The town of Waimea is horse country on Hawaii's Big Island, where *paniolos*, or Hawaiian cowboys, saddle up to work ranches and many people enjoy a life centered around horses. Here horses roam rolling fields and plains of gold and green grass, the trade winds blow, and majestic snowcapped Mauna Kea looms in the distance. Parker Ranch is an institution in Waimea, as it has had a huge impact on the development of the area and its culture.

Founded in 1847 by John Palmer Parker, the ranch is one of the largest in the United States, covering over 150,000 acres. Visitors can explore its plains and grasslands on horseback with Mauna Kea, a dormant volcano and Hawaii's highest peak, as a backdrop. On a clear day, the views of the mountain rising through clouds are fantastic.

Horses were first brought to Hawaii in 1803 by Captain Richard Cleveland, who gave them to King Kamehameha I as a gift. Kamehameha had also been given cattle. Both the horses and the cattle were set loose on the islands, and Kamehameha placed a *kapu*, or taboo, on the animals so that no one would harm them. The cattle quickly multiplied and became a problem, and Hawaiians grew to fear the wild, horned creatures that destroyed their lands. Kamehameha eventually asked John Parker—who brought the first musket to Hawaii—to take care of the cattle.

Parker obliged, selling their hides and salted beef while maintaining some cattle for himself. Parker also enlisted help, bringing in *vaqueros*, cowboys of Spanish and Mexican descent, to teach the locals how to rope and ride. These cowboys would impart many of their traditions to the local Hawaiians. Today, the *paniolos* have their own unique traditions that are distinctly Hawaiian. Being a *paniolo* can be a way of life, especially at a place like Parker Ranch.

The terrain at Parker Ranch looks like a vast range in Texas. In fact, except for the cinder cone in the distance, visitors may not believe that they are in Hawaii. Once on horseback, the different cowboy culture of the

islands comes to life, as the cool winds and the ever-shifting sky hint at quickly changing weather.

The nineteenth-century stone corrals of the ranch reveal how cattle were handled before the development of contemporary shipping standards. As many as 5,000 head of cattle would be driven down from the slopes of Mauna Kea and held in these corrals for shipping off the island. Cattle were then herded to the shores of the island, tied to the side of small craft, and rowed out to larger ships. The cattle literally swam for their lives, as they attempted not to swallow too much salt water en route to a larger boat. There, offshore in deep water, the cows that survived this journey were hoisted aboard by rope slings and taken to the mainland. This process was long and dangerous for cattle and cowboys alike.

To become a Parker Ranch cowboy, riders once had to mount bucking horses in the ranch's breaking pen and stay in the saddle. Those who failed could work other jobs. Those who succeeded on these dangerous rides gained the highly respected position of cowboy.

Today cowboys at the ranch still train horses, though the initiation process is not so rigorous. Only a dozen or so cowboys oversee the 250 horses and the 30,000 to 35,000 Angus and Charolais cattle on the ranch, working long days just as generations of cowboys did before them. Venturing out to see the cattle on horseback, one can begin to grasp the scale of this ranch and the scope of its influence on life in Waimea.

opposite Quarter horses greet riders in open pastures at Parker Ranch. It is thought that this American-bred horse is so named because during colonial times, it excelled at quarter-mile races. A versatile and fast breed with strong hindquarters, they are popular for ranch work across the United States.

pages 128–129 Riders pass fields of wetland taro, a Hawaiian staple starch rich in vitamins and minerals, in Waipi'o Valley. Taro needs fresh-flowing water, and this valley is an ideal place to cultivate the leafy plant.

above Beyond the corral where riders saddle up, Mauna Kea, the tallest mountain on the island, serves as Parker Ranch's backdrop. Mauna Kea is snowcapped for much of the winter; in the summer, one can make out the astronomical observatories on top.

The Valley of the Kings

Hawaii is the most isolated chain of islands on Earth, lying more than two thousand miles from North America. The Big Island offers an equally secluded destination, one surrounded by majestic two-thousand-foot cliffs dripping with waterfalls: Waipi'o Valley, the Valley of the Kings. Waipi'o is the southernmost of seven valleys that run in a chain along the Hamakua Coast. Many visitors stop at the lookout perched high on the southwestern ridge of the valley to observe Waipi'o and its black-sand beach. Some are wary of the hike down or do not want to risk their cars on the very steep, thin, paved valley road. Those who do venture down find a tropical wonderland fueled by *mana*, a sacred power, and the spirits of ancient Hawaii.

Many famous Hawaiian rulers spent time in Waipi'o Valley and remain buried in the valley walls, granting Waipi'o its designation as the Valley of the Kings. Legend has it that the first king of Hawaii, Kamehameha I, was hidden here as a baby. It may have been the simultaneous appearance of Halley's Comet that made those

around him believe that Kamehameha was destined for greatness. Kamehameha would fulfill this prophecy and go on to unite the Hawaiian Islands. Generations of his family would rule the islands for more than a century. Because of its sacred ancient burial mounds and temple sites, Waipi'o has strong spiritual significance for the native people of Hawaii.

Between the thirteenth and seventeenth centuries, thousands of Hawaiians made this fertile valley their home, living off the land and growing taro, a plant whose roots are crushed to make poi, a Hawaiian staple starch. In the late 1800s, horses were brought into the valley to help cultivate taro and do other work. This quiet farming community was devastated in 1946 when a tsunami swept through the valley, wreaking destruction and driving out most of the valley's residents. Between the tsunami and the displacement of horses by motor vehicles, Waipi'o's local herds were reduced to only a small wild group that locals call Hawaiian horses.

Some people believe that Hawaiian horses are the direct descendants of cow horses brought to the island by the *vaqueros*. Others in the valley maintain that the *vaqueros'* horses bred with a Quarter horse stallion that was released in the valley. Whatever their exact lineage, these horses are true survivors. It is not easy for these animals to live in such a wet and tropical place, but they do. A bit smaller than mainland breeds, Hawaiian horses roam casually through Waipi'o, unafraid of strange visitors or the few cars that descend into the valley. They are the only wild horses in the state of Hawaii.

At locally owned Na'alapa Stables, all but three of the horses used for trail rides are wild horses that were caught in the valley and trained. Their owners say Hawaiian horses are extraordinarily intelligent. They are also very vocal, whinnying to one another and perhaps to their relatives in the bands that inhabit the back of the valley.

The Hawaiian word *waipi'o* means "curved water." The floor of Waipi'o Valley is laced with small rivers, streams, and ponds, making hiking challenging and sometimes risky. The ready supply of fresh water made the valley an excellent place to cultivate taro and drew in the first Hawaiian settlers. It is easiest to navigate these streams and rivers on horseback with a local guide knowledgeable about the currents and the trails. The pathways hold natural surprises and wonders.

Near Na'alapa Stables, one may breathe in the sweet smell of plumeria trees, whose white flowers stand out in the green valley. After a few minutes of riding deeper into the valley down dirt roads, riders pass through what was once the central area when the valley was more populated. It was lined with a school, church, and rice mill. The road is now bounded by an old stone fence, thick vegetation, fruit trees, and a few small houses. It's difficult to imagine that thousands of people once lived in this now sparsely populated area. Along the way, one may pick fruit from an abundance of trees that line the road. Locals call this area the fruit orchard. Avocados the size of small footballs, exotic Chinese grapefruit, furry macadamia nuts, and greenish-yellow

star fruit abound. One may simply reach up to pick them while riding or get off and venture farther from the road amid the fruit trees. No trips to the farmers' market are required here; many simply live off the land, a quiet existence for those who desire one.

Past the orchard, the tree-lined dirt road opens up to spectacular views of the head of the valley. Here Hi'ilawe Falls cascades over one thousand feet down the valley wall. Hawaiian horses still live back here, as do the secrets of Hawaii's ancient rulers and their sacred valley.

opposite There is water everywhere in Waipi'o Valley. Residents who live here may have to drive through rivers to get to their homes. One may find oneself in a stream only to discover that it is someone's driveway.

above The only wild horse population in the state of Hawaii roams freely in Waipi'o Valley. Here a wild horse strolls along what locals call the fruit orchard. Both horses and humans can munch on an abundance of fruit grown in the valley—this lane is like a local farmers' market.

Kahua Ranch

Up Kohala Mountain Road on the northern tip of the Big Island, visitors are met by stunning views of the Kohala Coast framed by the high-country cacti that line the upper hills. The road winds to Kahua Ranch, a working cattle and sheep ranch where riders can let loose on horseback and experience the exhilaration of riding fast up high.

Kahua Ranch is in the Kohala Mountains, where an extinct volcano believed to be the oldest on the Big Island lies. The ranch dates back to 1928, when it was founded by Atherton Richards, a Honolulu business-man, and Ronald Von Holt, a rancher. Today it has approximately 3,300 Black Angus, Hereford, and Charolais mother cows that mill about paddocks with enviable views of the coast.

From the Kahua stables, riders climb up to a paddock to observe the cows in pastures kept green by frequent rains. At about four thousand feet above sea level, Kahua Ranch looks down upon a curve of the coast. It may seem from here that the Big Island is palpably growing—and in fact it is growing. The Big Island, the youngest of the Hawaiian islands, is constantly gaining land mass because of Kilauea, an active volcano that is said to be the home of Pele, Hawaii's volcano god-dess. Kilauea has been spewing lava—and creating new land—in a continuous eruption since 1983.

Riders can't escape vistas of the brilliantly blue Pacific far below, and they won't want to. At higher elevations in Waimea, they'll also encounter weather that changes quickly, bringing clouds, rain, and sunny blue skies all in the same hour. Farther up still, riders have the chance to canter and gallop into the clouds.

below Riders at Kahua Ranch, on the northern tip of the Big Island, venture through lush green hills on voyages that literally take them into the clouds. With guides from Na'alapa Stables, the outfitting company that leads rides at the ranch, riders can experience a fast ride on athletic horses.

opposite At about four thousand feet above sea level, Kahua Ranch looks down upon the Kohala Coast, the resort area of the Big Island. The weather up here is quite different from that of the warm and breezy coast: it's cool, windy, and wet, and conditions change quickly.

Contact Information

THE IRISH COAST
Omey Island
Cleggan Beach Riding Centre
Cleggan, Connemara
Co. Galway, Ireland
Telephone: +353 95 44746
www.clegganridingcentre.com
Riding to Omey Island.

Donegal
Donegal Language, Equestrian & Surf Centre
Bayshannon Road, Bundoran
Co. Donegal, Ireland
Telephone: +353 71 98 41977
www.donegalequestrianholidays.com
Riding on the beaches and Smuggler's Roads in Donegal.

The Cooley Peninsula
Ravensdale Lodge
Ravensdale, Dundalk
Co. Louth, Ireland
Telephone: +353 42 937 1034
www.ravensdalelodge.com
Riding in Ravensdale Forest.

The Ring of Kerry
Killarney Riding Stables
Ballydowney, Killarney
Co. Kerry, Ireland
Telephone: +353 64 31686
www.killarney-trail-riding.com
Riding around the Ring of Kerry.

The Connemara Pony
Dartfield Horse Museum
Dartfield, Killreekill, Loughrea
Co. Galway, Ireland
Telephone: +353 91 843 968
www.dartfieldhorsemuseum.net
Viewing Connemara ponies and horse history.

Aille Cross Equestrian Centre
Loughrea
Co. Galway, Ireland
Telephone: + 353 91 841216
www.connemara-trails.com
Riding Connemara ponies on the Connemara Trail.

THE IRISH COUNTRYSIDE
Mount Juliet Estate
Thomastown
Co. Kilkenny, Ireland
Telephone: +353 56 777 3000
www.mountjuliet.ie
Riding on the grounds of Mount Juliet.

The Irish National Stud
Tully, Kildare
Co. Kildare, Ireland
Telephone: + 353 45 521 251
www.irish-national-stud.ie
Thoroughbred horses, farm tour, and the Japanese Gardens.

County Clare
An Sibin Riding Centre
Mountshannon
Derryoran East, Whitegate
Co. Clare, Ireland
Telephone: +353 61 927411
www.irishhorseriding.com
Riding in County Clare.

ICELAND
Íshestar Riding Tours
Sörlaskeið 26
220 Hafnarfjörðr, Iceland
Telephone: +354-555-7000
www.ishestar.is
Gullfoss Horse Drive, riding outside Reykjavík, and all-around Icelandic horse tours.

SPAIN
Sevillá
Cortijo El Esparragal
Autovía A-66 Sevilla-Mérida
Gerena, Spain
Telephone: +34 95 578 27 02
www.elesparragal.com
Horseback riding on Andalusian horses on historic farm.

Doñana National Park
Centro Administrativo El AcebucheCalle El Pocito, 10
21730 - Almonte (Huelva), Spain
Telephone: +34 959 45 18 15
www.donana.es
Tours of Doñana National Park.

Segovia
Yeguada Centurión
Finca Santa Ana
Segovia, Spain
Telephone: +34 921 19 69 00
www.yeguadacenturion.com
Andalusian breeding farm with tours.

Jerez de la Frontera
Real Escuela Andaluza del Arte Ecuestre
Avda. Duque de Abrantes
11407 Jerez (Cádiz), Spain
Telephone: +34 956 31 96 35
www.realescuela.org
Horse show and museum.

Yeguada Real Tesoro
Ctra. Nacional IV, km. 640
Jerez de la Frontera, Spain
Telephone: + 34 95 632 1004
www.grupoestevez.es
Sherry bodega with black Andalusian horses.

THE GEORGIA COAST
Cumberland Island
Greyfield Inn
Cumberland Island, GA 31527
Telephone: 866-401-8581
www.greyfieldinn.com
Lodging on Cumberland Island.

Sea Island
P.O. Box 30351
Sea Island, GA 31561
Telephone: 888-SEA-ISLAND
www.seaisland.com
Nature tours, lessons, and beach riding.

Jekyll Island
Victoria's Carriage and Trail Rides
100 Stable Road
Jekyll Island, GA 31527
Telephone: 912-635-9500
Riding on Driftwood Beach.

THE CAROLINAS
Daufuskie Island
Daufuskie Island Resort & Breathe Spa
421 Squire Pope Road
Hilton Head, SC 29926
Telephone: 800-648-6778
www.daufuskieislandresort.com
Resort with equestrian center offering lessons in Western and English, trail rides, and carriage driving.

Cherokee
Cherokee Welcome Center
498 Tsali Boulevard
Cherokee, NC 28719
Telephone: 800-438-1601
www.cherokee-nc.com
Tourism office with information on riding in the Great Smoky Mountains, Oconaluftee Village, and other area attractions.

The Biltmore
The Biltmore Estate Equestrian Center
Biltmore, 1 Approach Road
Asheville, NC 28803
Telephone: 828-225-1454
www.biltmore.com
Lessons, clinics, and trail rides with an emphasis on Natural Horsemanship.

Inn on Biltmore Estate
1 Approach Road
Asheville, NC 28803
Telephone: 800-411-3812
www.biltmore.com/stay/inn
Accommodations for riders on the grounds of the Biltmore Estate.

VIRGINIA
Marriott Ranch
5305 Marriott Lane
Hume, VA 22639
Telephone: 877-324-7344
www.marriottranch.com
Western trail riding and cattle work on historic ranch.

The Virginia Steeplechase
Virginia Gold Cup
90 Main Street
Warrenton, VA 20186
Telephone: 800-69-RACES
www.vagoldcup.com
Steeplechase held each May. Open to the public.

Kelly's Ford
Inn at Kelly's Ford
16589 Edwards Shop Road
Remington, VA 22734
Telephone: 540-399-1779
www.innatkellysford.com
Guided horse tours and lessons at historic battlefield.

Middleburg
10 West Marshall Street
Middleburg, VA 20118
Telephone: 703-771-2170 ext. 11
www.VisitMiddleburg.org
Historic town with many equestrian-related offerings.

VERMONT
Mad River Valley
Vermont Icelandic Horse Farm
3061 North Fayston Road
Fayston, Vermont
Telephone: 802-496-7141
www.icelandichorses.com
Inn-to-inn ride on smooth-paced Icelandic horses.

Mountain Top Inn & Resort
195 Mountain Top Road
Chittenden, VT 05737
Telephone: 800-445-2100
www.mountaintopinn.com
Lessons and trail riding in the Green Mountains of Vermont.

University of Vermont Morgan Horse Farm
74 Battell Drive
Weybridge, VT 05753
Telephone: 802-388-2011
www.uvm.edu/morgan
Tours of historic Morgan breeding farm.

National Museum of the Morgan Horse
122 Bostwick Road
Shelburne, VT 05482
Telephone: 802-985-8665
www.morganmuseum.org/
Museum dedicated to Morgan horse history.

COLORADO
Northeastern Colorado Cattle Ranches
Colorado Cattle Company
70008 WCR 132
New Raymer, CO 80742
Telephone: 970-437-5345
www.coloradoduderanch.com
Working ranch offering cattle drives and special clinics.

San Juan National Forest
Rapp Corral
51 Haviland Lake Road
Durango, CO 81301
Telephone: 970-247-8454
www.rappcorral.com
Guided riding to Engineer Mountain and other parts of San Juan National Forest.

Wilderness Trails Ranch
1766 County Road 302
Durango, CO 81303
Telephone: 800-527-2624
www.wildernesstrails.com
Family ranch vacation in Durango, Colorado.

WYOMING
T Cross Ranch
P.O. Box 638
Dubois, WY 82513
Telephone: 877-827-6770
www.tcross.com
Dude ranch vacation.

Shoshone National Forest
UXU Ranch
1710 Yellowstone Highway
Wapiti, WY 82450
Telephone: 800-373-9027
www.uxuranch.com
Ranch vacation and riding in Shoshone National Forest.

Jackson Hole
Jackson Hole Horse Pack Fishing Trips
P.O. Box 9285
Jackson Hole, WY 83002
Telephone: 866-505-7007
www.fishjacksonwyo.com
Horse and fishing pack trips in Bridger-Teton National Forest.

Wild Mustangs
Red Canyon Wild Mustang Tours
1374 Sheridan Avenue
Cody, WY 82414-3733
Telephone: 800-293-0148
www.wildmustangtours.com
Tours to see the wild horses at McCullough Peaks.

CALIFORNIA WINE COUNTRY
Sonoma Vineyards
Wine Country Trail Rides
23355 Millerick Road
Sonoma, CA 95476
Telephone: 707-494-0499
www.vineyardrides.com
Riding at Larson Family Winery.

Redwoods
Armstrong Redwoods Pack Station
Box 287
Guerneville, CA 95446
Telephone: 707-887-2939
www.redwoodhorses.com
Guided horseback rides through redwoods at Armstrong Redwoods State Park.

Sugarloaf Ridge State Park
Triple Creek Horse Outfit
18995 Carriger Road
Sonoma, CA 95476
Telephone: 707-887-8700
www.triplecreekhorseoutfit.com
Guided horseback rides through Sugarloaf Ridge State Park.

MAUI
Haleakala
Pony Express Tours
P.O. Box 535, Haleakala Highway
Kula, HI 96790
Telephone: 808-667-2200
www.ponyexpresstours.com
Riding into Haleakala Crater.

Kipahulu
Maui Stables (Maui Horseback Tours)
P.O. Box 536
Kula, HI 96790
Telephone: 808-248-7799
www.mauistables.com
Guided rides into the rainforest and Haleakala National Park.

Makawao and Piiholo Ranch
Piiholo Ranch
Makawao
Maui, HI 96768
Telephone: 808-357-5544
www.piiholo.com
Riding in Upcountry Maui.

HAWAII'S BIG ISLAND
Parker Ranch
Cowboys of Hawaii
67-1435 Mamalahoa Highway
Kamuela, HI 96743
Telephone: 808-885-5006
www.cowboysofhawaii.com
Horseback riding on historic ranch in Waimea.

The Valley of the Kings
Na'alapa Stables
P.O. Box 437185
Kamuela, HI 96743
Telephone: 808-775-0419
www.naalapastables.com
Horseback riding into Waipi'o Valley.

Kahua Ranch
P.O. Box 837
Kamuela, HI 96743
Telephone: 808-882-4646
www.kahuaranch.com
A working ranch that welcomes visitors.

opposite Dale Clark leads a pack trip through Bridger-Teton National Forest outside Jackson Hole, Wyoming.

Index